BECOMING

a

WOMAN

of

DESTINY

JEREMY P. TARCHER/PENGUIN
a member of Penguin Group (USA) Inc.
New York

BECOMING

a

WOMAN

of

DESTINY

Turning Life's Trials

into Triumphs!

SUZAN JOHNSON COOK

JEREMY P. TARCHER/PENGUIN
Published by the Penguin Group
Penguin Group (USA) Inc., 375 Hudson Street, New York, New York 10014, USA
* Penguin Group (Canada), 90 Eglinton Avenue East, Suite 700,
Toronto, Ontario M4P 2Y3, Canada (a division of Pearson Canada Inc.) *
Penguin Books Ltd, 80 Strand, London WC2R 0RL, England * Penguin Ireland,
25 St Stephen's Green, Dublin 2, Ireland (a division of Penguin Books Ltd) *
Penguin Group (Australia), 250 Camberwell Road, Camberwell,
Victoria 3124, Australia (a division of Pearson Australia Group Pty Ltd) *
Penguin Books India Pvt Ltd, 11 Community Centre, Panchsheel Park,
New Delhi–110 017, India * Penguin Group (NZ), 67 Apollo Drive, Rosedale,
North Shore 0632, New Zealand (a division of Pearson New Zealand Ltd) *
Penguin Books (South Africa) (Pty) Ltd, 24 Sturdee Avenue, Rosebank,
Johannesburg 2196, South Africa

Penguin Books Ltd, Registered Offices: 80 Strand, London WC2R 0RL, England

Biblical passages throughout are taken from the King James, New International,
New Living Translation, New Revised Standard, and Douay-Rheims versions.

Most Tarcher/Penguin books are available at special quantity discounts for bulk purchase
for sales promotions, premiums, fund-raising, and educational needs. Special books or book
excerpts also can be created to fit specific needs. For details, write Penguin Group (USA)
Inc. Special Markets, 375 Hudson Street, New York, NY 10014.

Library of Congress Cataloging-in-Publication Data

Cook, Suzan Johnson.
Becoming a woman of destiny : turning life's trials into triumphs! / Suzan Johnson Cook.
p.   cm.
ISBN 978-1-58542-810-6
1. Women—Psychology.   2. Women heroes.   I. Title.
HQ1206.C698   2010   2010023071
248.8'43—dc22

Printed in the United States of America
1   3   5   7   9   10   8   6   4   2

BOOK DESIGN BY AMANDA DEWEY

While the author has made every effort to provide accurate telephone numbers and Internet
addresses at the time of publication, neither the publisher nor the author assumes any
responsibility for errors, or for changes that occur after publication. Further, the publisher
does not have any control over and does not assume any responsibility for author or third-
party websites or their content.

In loving memory of
DOROTHY C. JOHNSON, my mom.
This is the moment you prepared me for.

And in honor of Destiny women

Michelle Obama, First Lady of the U.S.A., and your mom;

Secretary Hillary Rodham Clinton and Justice Sonia Sotomayor;

Oprah Winfrey and Maya Angelou;

Meg Armstrong, my Life Coach;

Donna Hicks Izzard, Gini Booth, Dr. Katie Cannon, and
Mercedes Nesfield, my loyal Destiny Friends, who laughed, loved,
prayed, and stayed with me all the way.

And to Wilbert T. Johnson, my Destiny dad,
who sacrificed so my dreams and destiny could live.

CONTENTS

PILLAR II.
SPIRITUALITY

PILLAR III.
ACTION

PILLAR IV.
COMMUNITY

And Deborah, a prophetess, the wife of Lapidoth, she judged
Israel at that time. And she dwelt under the palm tree of Deborah
between Ramah and Beth-el in mount Ephraim: and the children of
Israel came up to her for judgment.

—Judges 4:4–5 (KJV)

The Woman of Destiny's Prayer

God,

Thank you for creating me woman.

Thank you for teaching me how to give and receive love.

Please go before me, to show me the way.

Please go behind me, to push me with your divine touch.

Please watch over me, that I may be covered in your
unconditional love.

Most of all, please give me wisdom to walk the paths that you
have blazed and ordained for me, and to know the
difference between right and wrong.

I invite you inside me that I may have your anointing.

I seek you everywhere that I may know your fullness.

Teach me to make wise choices in every area of my life.

Surround me with and keep me in the midst of other wise women.

Give me the clarity to share the wisdom I have to impart
to women who seek to be wise themselves.

Thank you for creating me woman.

I am blessed and highly favored.

I am a Woman of Destiny.

I am making Destiny Decisions.

I am destined for greatness!

ACKNOWLEDGMENTS

I always thank God first, for creating and blessing me with marvelous parents, family, and extended family. So this is first a tribute to Dorothy and Wilbert T. Johnson, who took me to church and introduced me to the biblical Deborah and the modern-day Deborahs, who affirmed that the palace, not the "pit," was my destiny; and to my family, especially my two sons, Samuel and Christopher, who lived so patiently with this mother as her destiny unfolded, and Ron, who helped me change cartridges when I was technologically challenged and who cooked so our kids could eat. (You really are the better cook.)

What a marvelous journey this has been, to have an amazing literary agent, Lois de la Haba, who made introductions to two of the finest people in the world, Joel Fotinos and Antonia Felix. Thank you for understanding me, investing in me, and recognizing and acknowledging the gifts that were inside me, shouting to come out and be seen and heard. And to Meg Armstrong, who helped prepare me to confidently "walk into the room."

And to the many amazing women in my life: Brenda Richardson, Melody Martin, my Jack & Jill sisters, my Sag Harbor sisters, and my Wisdom Women Worldwide circle of sisters, who all help me keep my balance as well as my focus, and help me to just have good old fun, and Secretary of State Hillary Rodham Clinton, an extraordinary woman. To the men who listened and cheered me on: my late brother Charles Ronald Johnson; Dr. James A. Forbes; Dr. Gardner Taylor, who named me "the Harriet Tubman for women ministers"; and my spiritual "dads," Dad Mason, Dad Vaughn, and Bishop John R. Bryant.

This book is not only about becoming a Woman of Destiny, but also about achieving your destined success. While writing it my life was in transition, which is another message to Women of Destiny and "ladies in waiting"—that every season we are in is full of potential and should not be negated nor denied. Go through and flow through the season you are in right now. It may have challenges and cry out for change, but you will get through it. Life is supposed to be this way—not so much for everyone outside to look in but for you to look inside out, digging deeply into your destiny wells, making Destiny Decisions, and evolving into the woman God desires you to be. What an exciting time—to witness those who have reached their Divinely destined places—Oprah Winfrey and Barbara Walters, the Destiny women of broadcasting; Secretary Hillary Rodham Clinton and Justice Sonia Sotomayor from my "homeland," New York; and to watch with amazement those in entertainment, such as Queen Latifah and our beloved author Maya Angelou, whose writings have demonstrated what destiny looks, lives, and feels like. Thank you, our Queens, for modeling it—molding it and letting it unfold right before our eyes.

My dear Destiny sisters, close the chapters that need to be closed in your life and allow new and exciting ones to open, just as you do when you open, close, and flip the pages of this book. Enjoy life. Do not be destroyed by it. You will find peace of mind. You will expand your reach and broaden your horizons. You will cry again. You will smile again. You will have night sweats and daydreams. You will be blown away when you find that, "Wow, this is the moment I've been waiting for. I've found my place." It may take many Destiny Decisions to get there, but once you've arrived, you'll know it.

Amazingly, as this book is released, I've found my Destiny place—and I know it!

May you enjoy reading and participating in this book as much as I have enjoyed writing it.

FOREWORD

Before I attended a service by Dr. Sujay, as she is affectionately known to many, I thought I had a good idea of the variety of American religious experience. Both my husband and I were familiar with many denominations through our upbringings in Lutheran and Congregational churches and our "church jobs," work as professional soloists and choral section leaders in churches in the Midwest and New York City. So when a friend told me about a new type of service in Harlem, I was curious. I had always wanted to see the Apollo Theater anyway, and visiting the historic venue to witness a completely new style of "church" was too intriguing to pass up.

It was . . . amazing. Dancers swept across the stage in flowing costumes and moves that expressed the radiance of inspired life, a high-powered African-American woman executive spoke about the power of faith, a women's chorus from Japan lit the air with song, and a brilliant neurosurgeon with a new book took interview questions from Dr. Sujay. The combination of historic setting, large crowd, variety of presentations, and Dr. Sujay's electric and graceful presence made the service one of the most moving hours I had ever spent. There was so much love in that big red velvet place that I thought we would all melt into the floor.

Dr. Sujay's talent for preaching and connecting to an audience came through on that stage, but what struck me most were the words she did not say, the vision behind her production that knew what her diverse audience needed. She pulled together an event that addressed thinking people, creative people, and curious people. Those like so many I know who were brought up in church but who no longer felt that every line of the dogma represented their vibrant spirituality. I've been fortunate to become a friend of Dr. Sujay, and knowing her has confirmed the vision I saw manifested at the Apollo. She understands the range of our spiritual attitudes and is strongly committed to helping people from all walks of life, especially women, explore their full potential—intellectual, creative, and spiritual.

The course Dr. Sujay maps out in this book, which connects women to the traits they share with Deborah, the superwoman of the Old Testament, promises rich experiences for women entering their mature years. Her message is loud and clear: Your best work is still ahead of you.

—Antonia Felix
Author of *Sonia Sotomayor: The True American Dream*

PREFACE

Women entering their mature years, after they have built their careers, raised their families, and reached the goals that define their place in the world, face a whole new set of challenges. When I turned fifty, I realized that the rules and advice that had been such important guides to my success were geared to young people who have a world of experiences ahead of them. Where is the rulebook, I asked myself, for women with a wealth of experience *behind* them? What dreams have been simmering throughout my life, waiting for the day I can give them my full attention and the priceless riches of my experience? In other words, how do I step into the rest of my life?

The answers to those questions fill the pages of *Becoming a Woman of Destiny.*

As a professional woman with a career in the church and public policy, I needed mentoring that recognized my gifts as an experienced, intelligent, ambitious, and spiritual woman of the world. After thirty years of preaching, I knew it was time to take my passion for speaking to a new platform. My vocation had taken me to exciting and fulfilling heights, including a job in the White House, but I was anxious to take the next leap.

Then I remembered Deborah, the prophetess from the Old Testament. I reread her story in Judges and found the role model for myself and all my women friends who were stepping into a new season of life. Her song in Judges 5 seemed to call out to me personally: "Awake, awake, [and] utter a song!"

My song is this book, a guide for women in transition due to economic changes, divorce, children raised and gone, retirement, or simply a sense that it is time to step into a personal journey with like-minded women.

The story of Deborah from the Old Testament book of Judges describes a woman unique in all biblical history. Not only was she a **prophetess** who relayed the divine word of God to the people, she was also a **judge**, a wise counselor who settled disputes and held the elevated position of a heroine and leader in her society. In addition, Deborah fulfilled the role of a **warrior** who led her troops into battle and freed them from enemies who had violently oppressed them for twenty years. These qualities combined with Deborah's role as a **wife** to make her an icon among women of ancient history, a figure whom one scholar calls "the ideal woman."

Each quality that Deborah exhibited stands as a beacon for contemporary women who seek to grow into their highest potential. Deborah was a woman of astute and practical intelligence, spirituality, integrity, and action. These attributes make up the Four Pillars of a life committed to exciting new goals and priorities. My name for those who stride into periods of transition with Deborah's wisdom and power is Women of Destiny. They draw on the priceless skills, insights, and experience of the first half of their lives to launch into a new season of creativity and productivity.

I am not the first to discover the powerful effects of Deborah's story. Queen Elizabeth I was compared to Deborah as a brilliant, confident, and powerful leader. Narratives about Deborah were popular in her time, where entire pageants were devoted to her. In a time and place in which so little of women's lives were under their own control, Elizabethan women looked to Deborah to remind them of their strength and depth of faith—and God's gender-blindness.

Deborah speaks just as powerfully in our time. She is ready to lead us into the fulfillment of roles and activities for which we have been preparing our entire lives.

This book is a guide to becoming a Woman of Destiny, determined, destined, and not distracted. Her determination comes through as she takes the time to listen to her heart and uncover the gifts she wants to develop. She carefully assesses these goals and strategizes a plan for achieving them, boldly and joyfully moving toward her new destiny. Along the way, she develops a closer relationship with God to become, like Deborah, a multifaceted woman who is wise in mind and spirit. No longer distracted by the obstacles that prevented her from working on her most heart-felt desires, she creates a new life with more to give to her own well-being and potential, her friends and family, and the world.

Throughout my five decades of life as a wife, mother, educator, minister, and public speaker, I have been blessed to have a number of wise women at my side to guide and inspire me. The first was my mother, Dorothy C. Johnson, at whose feet I first learned about a woman's strength of body, mind, and spirit. When I attended seminary, learning about Deborah added more dimensions to the template for my life journey, ushering me into an awareness of what I—and every woman—can do, if we try to live up to her code.

Each chapter in this book is devoted to a method for developing Deborah's qualities, rounded out with anecdotes from my life and those of others that illustrate each area of development in a modern, practical way.

By integrating Deborah's qualities in the order presented, you will realize more of your potential and launch a new phase of your life with confidence, generosity, wisdom, and the encouragement of your own Destiny Circle, a group of women dedicated to becoming Women of Destiny.

Chapter One

DEBORAH

The Original Woman of Destiny

O
f all the heroes and heroines of biblical history, only one held the combined roles of judge, military strategist, poet, and prophet. Not even King David could claim that entire mix of power and leadership. Deborah was that astonishing figure, a wise, brave, respected, and divinely inspired leader who ruled with both earthly and heavenly powers.

Commissioned by God, Deborah took her place as a leader of ancient Israel at a time of crisis when the people needed someone to deliver them from a brutally oppressive enemy. The only woman in the Bible ever to hold the post of judge—the leadership role in place before Israel had kings—Deborah had enormous responsibility as the political and spiritual guide of her people. No biblical woman before or after Deborah had been given that power. To fulfill her duties, Deborah had to possess keen intelligence and a thorough knowledge of the law and be decisive, creative, diplomatic, confident, comfortable with giving orders, and receptive to the voice of God. As one biblical scholar put it, "A woman of her stature never reappears in biblical literature."

> *As an authoritative leader and a prophet, it is appropriate to portray Deborah as a "woman of torches," someone burning with intellectual and spiritual energy.*

Deborah lived and ruled about eight miles north of Jerusalem between the villages of Rama and Bethel. Judges 4:5 states that "she dwelt under the palm tree of Deborah" in the hilly region called Mount Ephraim "and the children of Israel came up to her for judgment." According to descriptions in the Old Testament, judges were "raised up" by God to the position, acted as spiritual guides by teaching about God and God's law, listened to cases and administered justice, tried to prevent idol worship, and led the people into war. Stationed in the hill country north of Jerusalem, Deborah was a vital force of justice and spiritual guidance. People were drawn to her public "courtroom" to resolve cases that were too difficult to settle themselves and to listen to her wisdom on the law of Moses and to the voice of God that came through her.

Deborah's stature was all the more amazing because of the culture in which she lived. Women in ancient Israel were virtually legal non-persons and their primary role was to bear children. They were not allowed to be priests or to even attend the annual religious celebrations due to the "ritual uncleanliness" of menstruation and childbirth. As Alice Ogden Bellis explains in *Helpmates, Harlots, and Heroes,* Deborah's realm was truly a man's world:

> The basic unit in Hebrew society was the family, headed by the father; it was called "the father's house." The religious community in turn was made up of adult males, all those who had been circumcised. These are the people of Israel, who are also the warriors. This community shaped the laws that aimed to preserve the integrity of the family, where the family is frequently identified with its male head. Laws protect the man's rights against external and internal threats. Rarely were laws concerned with dependents' rights.

Confronting problems as opportunities for growth is one of Deborah's great lessons for women today, and it is part of the path toward becoming a Woman of Destiny.

The Deborah We Know

Deborah's dramatic story is told in Judges 4 and 5, where she is described as a judge, prophet, and the wife of Lapidot. The Hebrew words of that name, *eshet lapidot*, which could mean "woman of lapidot" or, literally, "woman of torches," give us layers of meaning about Deborah's personality. The association with torches leads some scholars to describe Deborah as a "fiery" or "spirited" woman. As an authoritative leader and a prophet, it is appropriate to portray Deborah as a "woman of torches," someone burning with intellectual and spiritual energy.

> *No matter how patriarchal the culture of her time, it could not deny the Lord's use of her. When God chose, patriarchalism had to give way.*
>
> —*Denise Carmody*, Biblical Women: Contemporary Reflections on Biblical Texts

The palm tree in Deborah's story also tells us something about the nature of her authority. There were no palms in the forested hills of Mount Ephraim, so the writer may have chosen this type of tree for the symbolic meaning it gave to Deborah's place of power. The famous Bible commentator John Wesley wrote that

Deborah's palm was "an emblem of the justice she administered there: thriving and growing against opposition, as the palm-tree does under pressures." Always pictured beneath the shadow of a palm tree, Deborah takes on the personality of a woman who is at her best when faced with challenges, obstacles, and tough decisions. Challenges make her stronger, brighter, and expanded in wisdom. Confronting problems as opportunities for growth is one of Deborah's great lessons for women today, and it is part of the path toward becoming a Woman of Destiny.

Deborah's tree also represents a place of contemplation where we can sort out our priorities and decide how to best manage our time. For many women of all ages, from career women who are raising families to more mature women whose personal and professional responsibilities seem to expand by the year, layers of obligations make it difficult to master time management. Deborah is a model of calm and stability, inviting us to give everything its due season.

The wisdom that each part of life has its own season is a valuable lesson of Deborah's story. As a judge, she had to take time to sit back and listen and then integrate and step up to make judgments. Those alternating phases of being receptive and proactive mirrored her role as a prophet, in which she listened to God and then acted on the messages by either relating them to the people or following the directions she had been given to make war on the enemy.

The cycles of life are also reflected in the background to Deborah's story. During the period of Judges (about 1050–1000 BC), the tribes of Israel went through a pattern of virtuous living followed by a decline that caused them to fall victim to enemies. God would hear their cries and send a judge to defeat the enemy and rally the people back to a lawful and Godly life. That judge's act of deliverance would then be followed by forty years of peace. When the people gradually fell into bad ways once again, the cycle repeated. This speaks to us because as Women of Destiny entering an exciting new phase of life, we know that we will make mistakes and that there will always be help to lead us forward. We may have to return to one particular lesson time after time, but we will become stronger and more compassionate along the way.

Our lives are filled with cycles, and a Woman of Destiny transitions into new phases with novel approaches to territory she has mastered before, such as learning, integrating, building "family," and sharing her gifts with others. The work we've done up until now has borne much fruit, but the work we do in our new season uses all the wisdom and experience we have gained to take our lives to a new level. We have new missions, roles, passions, and priorities, and many more resources at our disposal than before to support them.

The great thing about getting older is that you don't lose all the other ages you've been.

⤛ ⤜

—*Madeleine L'Engle, award-winning author*

In the time of Judges, which came after the Israelites' exodus out of Egypt, "there was no king in Israel; every man did that which was right in his own eyes," according to Judges 17:6 (KJV). Deborah's prominent role as a beacon of justice and Godliness when many of the tribes of Israel were estranged from each other and there was no official government or monarchy holding them together made her God's chosen "deliverer" at a critical time. Deborah's call to action came after the Canaanites of the north had taken over the land previously conquered by Joshua.

King Jabin, who ruled the Canaanites from the city of Hazor in the northern region of Galilee, had a massive army led by a general named Sisera. With nine hundred war chariots, Sisera's troops had terrorized the northern region for twenty years, making it impossible for the Israelites to live in open villages or travel the main roads. The iron-made horse-drawn chariots were dreaded machines of war, which biblical scholars believe were outfitted with razor-sharp scythes jutting out from each axle. The Israelites, with few weapons of their own, were defenseless against these chariots and Sisera's ruthless army.

Barely able to stay alive in the hills, they cried out to God for help and God responded through Deborah.

Using her commanding authority, Deborah called for an Israelite warrior named Barak ("Thunderbolt") to come to her to receive a message from God. She told Barak that he must gather a ten-thousand-man army from among the tribes of Israel and bring them to Mount Tabor near the Sea of Galilee. Barak listened as Deborah spoke for God: "I will lure Sisera, the commander of Jabin's army, with his chariots and his troops to the Kishon River and give him into your hands." The Kishon River could be seen from the top of Mount Tabor as it cut across valley's flat Plain of Megiddo that spread out below the mountain.

God's plan was clear: Barak's army would wait at the top of Mount Tabor for Sisera's troops to march into the valley below. When the enemies battled, God would make Barak the victor. The battle plan had come from the highest authority, God's prophetess, but Barak hesitated. The odds were outrageous and he was not willing to go into battle without a good-luck charm. He said to Deborah, "If thou wilt go with me, then I will go: but if thou wilt not go with me, then I will not go."

Deborah agreed to join Barak, but in response to his lack of faith she immediately relayed another prophetic message: "At this time the victory shall not be attributed to thee, because Sisera shall be delivered into the hand of a woman." Barak would win the battle, but he would not get credit for killing the famed general Sisera.

Deborah inspired Barak and his men with her divine authority and fiery, unwavering faith, and the militia marched down the mountain toward the valley.

Rallied by Deborah, Barak gathered an army from several tribes and with each addition the troops became more embold-

ened for the mission. This was a major turning point for the Israelites, who had not bonded together since leaving Egypt. "For the
first time in its history," wrote Reverend G. A. Cooke, "Israel acts
in a national capacity; it was the genius and courage of Deborah
that instigated this united action."

> *With each addition the troops became more*
> *emboldened for the mission. . . . "It was the*
> *genius and courage of Deborah that instigated*
> *this united action."*

With fearless determination, Deborah marched with the army
to the top of Mount Tabor, where they made camp. Sisera heard
about the movement of these forces and sent his troops and chariots to the sprawling valley below the mountain, exactly as Deborah's prophecy said he would. We can imagine how terrified Barak
and his troops must have been to look down and see Sisera's nine
hundred chariots and huge army gathered in the valley, waiting
for them. How were they supposed to defeat these well-armed
soldiers and deadly chariots? But with Deborah alongside him,
Barak was certain that God would somehow "deliver" Sisera into
his hands. The doubt and hesitation that struck him at the beginning of Deborah's call never returned.

When everything was in place, Deborah once again spoke
for God and gave Barak the order to attack: "Arise, for this is

the day wherein the Lord hath delivered Sisera into thy hands." She never hesitated or questioned her gift, but completely trusted God's messages and acted on them. Deborah inspired Barak and his men with her divine authority and fiery, unwavering faith, and the militia marched down the mountain toward the valley.

Bravely facing Sisera's troops and chariots, Barak's foot soldiers could not imagine how they could win against the advancing army. But suddenly the sky grew dark with thick clouds and a devastating storm blew into the valley. "War from heaven was made against them" and God threw Sisera's troops into wild confusion. The horses panicked and the soldiers that were not killed by the rampage of chariots tried to run away. Armed with swords, Barak's men charged headlong into the madness "and all the host of Sisera fell upon the edge of the sword; and there was not a man left." The Kishon River flooded and swept away the bodies, while "the stoutest of the enemies fled," including Sisera.

The terrorized general escaped on foot and reached the tents of a Kenite clan. An Arab tribe, the Kenites were friendly with Israel and had also made peace with the Canaanites. Heber the Kenite knew and was on good terms with King Jabin, so Sisera went to the tent of Heber's wife, Jael. She recognized the general and invited him in: "Turn in, my lord, turn in to me; fear not." He asked her for water and she showed him respect by giving him milk instead, and spread a blanket over him. Sisera told Jael to stand watch by the opening of her tent so that if anyone came and asked if there was a man in her tent, she could say no and send them away. Exhausted from the battle and his flight from the valley, Sisera fell asleep.

Jael's next move fulfilled the prophecy Deborah had announced to Barak. She picked up a hammer and a long, sharp tent stake and quietly crouched down by Sisera's head. Carefully placing the tip of the stake on his temple, she pounded it through his head so hard that it not only killed him but pinned his head to the ground. Barak, who had been racing after Sisera, arrives at the tent and Jael shows him in: "Come, and I will shew thee the man whom thou seekest," she says in Judges 4:22 (KJV). "And when he came into her tent, behold, Sisera lay dead, and the nail was in his temples."

Like Deborah, Jael broke the mold: Women were supposed to be prizes of war, not warriors who took it into their own hands to end twenty years of tyranny. "Blessed among women be Jael the wife of Haber the Kenite, and blessed be she in her tent," sings Deborah.

> *Like Deborah, Jael broke the mold: Women were supposed to be prizes of war, not warriors who took it into their own hands to end twenty years of tyranny.*

In her poem in Judges 5, Deborah highlights the irony of a woman killing Sisera by flashing us into the scene of Sisera's home, where his mother is fretting at the window. "Why is his chariot so long in coming back?" she wonders. "Why are the feet of his horses so slow?" One of Sisera's wives tells her that he is probably busy dividing the spoils, gathering up clothes and furniture and "the fairest of the women." By bringing in those women's perspectives, Deborah's poem stands out among other ancient biblical verse. "Amid all the jubilation, the triumphant nationalism of Deborah's poem," wrote Norah Lofts in *Women in the Old Testament*, "there is something too often ignored, something that is absent from much of biblical poetry—an introspective approach to the defeated."

After the battle against Sisera's army by Deborah, Barak, and Jael, the tribes of Israel enjoyed forty years of peace.

The poetic version of the story, Deborah and Barak's victory song in Judges 5, is one of the oldest writings in the Bible, along with another woman's poem, Miriam's "Song at the Sea" in Exodus. Great poems and psalms go hand-in-hand with famous leaders of the Old Testament, and Deborah's poem celebrates that she arose "a mother in Israel" to take care of her broken and demoralized people. The victory she prophesied and helped carry out is so magnificent that she must sing about it and declare the wonder of God who gave her, a woman, such a high position: "Awake, awake, Deborah: awake, awake, utter a song . . . the Lord made me have dominion over the mighty."

Deborah stood proudly in her role as leader and prophet. Everyone depended on her—men, women, and children, including a great military leader and his ten thousand men—and she led with spirit and confidence. She was a revered model of sound judgment, faith in God, and, as a prophet—God's hotline to the people—the object of awe. Deborah has no peers in history, but her breathtaking portrait gives us a guidebook to live by as strong, confident Women of Destiny.

> *Deborah has no peers in history, but her breathtaking portrait gives us a guidebook to live by as strong, mature Women of Destiny.*
>
> ⌒∾

DEBORAH'S FOUR-PILLARED MODEL FOR WOMEN OF DESTINY

A Woman of Destiny is called to build upon her hard-earned wisdom and experience to reach a new level of personal greatness. Drawing on specific qualities from Deborah's life, we can follow a fourfold path that leads us to the destiny we are ready to fulfill in the new season of our lives. The four pillars of this journey to becoming a Woman of Destiny—**Intelligence, Spirituality, Action, and Community**—mirror the qualities that Deborah brought to her life and work.

Pillar I: Intelligence. This characteristic of Deborah invites us to pursue new goals with clarity, decisiveness, and thoughtful strategies. Entering a new season of life, a Woman of Destiny turns to dreams and goals that may have been put off as she raised a family and/or cultivated a career. Just as Deborah rallied to the call of battle, you take specific actions to map out and fulfill your new goals. As an apprentice of wisdom, you take the time to discover your most deeply held dreams and envision how you want to spend your energy and resources in the next chapter of your life.

The four pillars of the journey to becoming a Woman of Destiny—Intelligence, Spirituality, Action, and Community—mirror the qualities that Deborah brought to her life and work.

Being organized, making well-informed and analyzed choices, and drawing up step-by-step plans is an intelligent way to move ahead to get results. Difficult choices must be made in order to move out of comfort zones and break new ground.

Another aspect of a Woman of Destiny that reflects Deborah's intelligence is the ability to embrace hardship as opportunity. After defining your calling and setting up a strategy for turning it into reality, you learn how to approach the obstacles that will inevitably get in the way. Deborah's responsibility as a judge included settling disputes, giving wise counsel, and teaching people the law of the land. Like Deborah, a woman entering any new season of her life recognizes the valuable lesson hiding within every challenge. You see problems as opportunities to learn, develop, and stretch yourself beyond your current boundaries of knowledge and experience. Deborah's successful military campaign led to forty years of peace for all the tribes of Israel. One of the hallmarks of a Woman of Destiny's intelligence is knowing that every challenge is there for your ultimate good. This attitude also makes room for more joy and fun in your life. Rather than being bogged down by anxiety and worries, you are grateful for the brightness in the smallest moments of everyday life. You see the beauty and feel the joy of being alive at work and play.

> *A Woman of Destiny sees problems as opportunities to learn, develop, and stretch yourself beyond your current boundaries of knowledge and experience.*

Pillar II: Spirituality. The pillar of spirituality takes you on a path of nurturing your sacred self through prayer and trust in God. A Woman of Destiny knows the power of communing with God because she has been both the giver and receiver of effective prayer. Judges in ancient Israel prayed for the people. Like

Deborah, we should consider it a sacred responsibility to pray for ourselves and everyone in our lives. By developing this relationship with God, we forge a deeper commitment to the spiritual center of our being, and this commitment propels us in new directions, both within and without. A Woman of Destiny realizes that wholeness comes from drawing upon our mental, emotional, and spiritual qualities to inform everything we do.

Deborah is truly a woman in a position of power in the world of men. . . . Deborah assumes a very masculine role when she "sent and summoned Barak" to come to her. Though women may indeed direct male activities, I cannot think of another instance when a woman demands a man respond to her command in this tone.

—*Lillian R. Klein,* From Deborah to Esther: Sexual Politics in the Hebrew Bible

As a prophetess, Deborah was God's mouthpiece and the people revered her for it. All women can listen to God's voice by showing the same reverence for their intuition, their God-given connection to the Holy Spirit, universal intelligence, discernment, or whatever you choose to call it. Intuition, which I like to call "spiritual intelligence," is designed to help your decision-making ability, provide answers on every imaginable subject, and guide you in the direction for your best possible good. A Woman of Destiny pays attention to subtle "nudges," messages and signals that help to plug in to this vast source of information.

Pillar III: Action. Deborah's proactive personality is reflected in the pillar of action, which emphasizes performing every action with integrity and infusing the world with the fruits of your new wisdom. As you pursue your goals with your mind and spirit in balance, you behave and relate to others with the highest ethical standards. Deborah followed the tradition of judges as spelled out in the days of Moses, treating everyone equally, never taking bribes and honoring the situation of the person with the one-dollar problem as much as the one with the million-dollar complaint. Her fairness and honesty were the only light in a dark and chaotic place, and we can bring the same radiance to everything we do. Now more than ever, the world needs women who aren't afraid to walk the talk about doing the right thing.

> *Now more than ever, the world needs women who aren't afraid to walk the talk about doing the right thing.*

The second element of action in Pillar III is giving back. Deborah was comfortable with her power and her role as a leader. As a

Woman of Destiny you use the strength, insights, and knowledge you have developed to enrich the world by achieving your goals and bringing your gifts to the world. Armed with Deborah's multifaceted intelligence, clear-cut strategies for turning dreams into reality, and rich spiritual life, you embark on a larger mission with projects, speeches, programs, art, lectures, political work, activism, or conferences to put their wisdom into practice. You forge ahead to deliver the books that need to be written, photographs that need to be taken, classes that need to be attended, or movies and plays that need to be produced.

Pillar IV: Community. The final step of developing the nature of a Woman of Destiny is forming your Destiny Circle. This group is an essential laboratory where women learn from each other's life experiences, measure their progress, validate their work and ideas, and find encouragement and inspiration. The Destiny Circle is a serious place to nurture and be nurtured, to draw on the lifelong lessons and collective knowledge of other women with the same desire to move into an enriching and productive new chapter of their lives.

Those further along the Woman of Destiny path are mentors to others, and every member can trust that the issues and ideas shared in the Destiny Circle remain solely within the group. The circle is a safe, confidential place set apart from work, home, therapist's office, salon, or church. From stay-at-home mothers to professionals, women in all walks of life need a place to realize their personal growth without being pulled into the demands and constraints of various institutions and organizations.

. . .

LIKE DEBORAH, Women of Destiny use their intelligence and talents to their fullest ability, act with confidence, live spiritually, and are not afraid to march into unknown territory. Developing each of those qualities guarantees that Women of Destiny will experience a new season of life filled with exceptional achievements in every imaginable field, from business to foundations to the arts, to enrich the world like no one else can. As the opening verses in *Female Excellency, or the Ladies Glory*, a seventeenth-century book about Deborah and other heroines, claimed, Deborah was among the first to prove that strong women have great work to do:

It's evident that Woman can
Equal if not Exceed the Deeds of Man.

The biblical story of Deborah is found in Judges 4 and 5, and there are a few differences in the accounts. The poem, which makes up Judges 5, is much older than Judges 4 and is considered one of the most ancient texts in the Old Testament. In the "Song of Deborah," as the poem is known, Deborah describes how she was called to lead the people ("a mother arose in Israel"), describes the battle against the Canaanites, celebrates the victory over General Sisera, praises the Israelites who put their lives on the line to go into battle against this terrifying enemy, criticizes those who did not, describes in detail how Jael killed Sisera (with details that differ from the story in Judges 4), and creates a scene about Sisera's family.

THE SONG OF DEBORAH

JUDGES 5

(Douay-Rheims Version)

1 In that day Debbora and Barac son of Abinoem sung, and said:

2 O you of Israel, that have willingly offered your lives to danger, bless the Lord.

3 Hear, O ye kings, give ear, ye princes: It is I, it is I, that will sing to the Lord, I will sing to the Lord the God of Israel.

4 O Lord, when thou wentest out of Seir, and passedst by the regions of Edom, the earth trembled, and the heavens dropped water.

5 The mountains melted before the face of the Lord, and Sinai before the face of the Lord the God of Israel.

6 In the days of Samgar the son of Anath, in the days of Jahel the paths rested: and they that went by them, walked through by-ways.

7 The valiant men ceased, and rested in Israel: until Debbora arose, a mother arose in Israel.

8 The Lord chose new wars, and he himself overthrew the gates of the enemies: a shield and spear was not seen among forty thousand of Israel.

9 My heart loveth the princes of Israel: O you that of your own good will offered yourselves to danger, bless the Lord.

10 Speak, you that ride upon fair asses, and you that sit in judgment, and walk in the way.

11 Where the chariots were dashed together, and the army of the enemies was choked, there let the justices of the Lord be rehearsed, and his

clemency towards the brave men of Israel: then the people of the Lord went down to the gates, and obtained the sovereignty.

12 Arise, arise, O Debbora, arise, arise, and utter a canticle. Arise, Barac, and take hold of thy

captives, O son of Abinoem.

13 The remnants of the people are saved, the Lord hath fought among the valiant ones.

14 Out of Ephraim he destroyed them into Amalec, and after him out of Benjamin into thy people, O Amalec: Out of Machir there came down princes, and out of Zabulon they that led the army to fight.

15 The captains of Issachar were with Debbora, and followed the steps of Barac, who exposed himself to danger, as one going headlong, and into a pit. Ruben being divided against himself, there was found a strife of courageous men.

16 Why dwellest thou between two borders, that thou mayest hear the bleatings of the flocks? Ruben being divided against himself, there was found a strife of courageous men.

17 Galaad rested beyond the Jordan, and Dan applied himself to ships: Aser dwelt on the sea shore, and abode in the havens.

18 But Zabulon and Nephtali offered their lives to death in the region of Merome.

19 The kings came and fought, the kings of Chanaan fought in Thanach by the waters of Mageddo, and yet they took no spoils.

20 War from heaven was made against them, the stars remaining in their order and courses fought against Sisara.

21 The torrent of Cison dragged their carcasses, the torrent of Cadumim, the torrent of Cisoii: tread thou, my soul, upon the strong ones.

22 The hoofs of the horses were broken whilst the stoutest of the enemies fled amain, and fell headlong down.

23 Curse ye the land of Meroz, said the angel of the Lord: curse the inhabitants thereof, because they came not to the help of the Lord, to help his most valiant men.

24 Blessed among women be Jahel the wife of Haber the Cinite, and blessed be she in her tent.

25 He asked her water and she gave him milk, and offered him butter in a dish fit for princes.

26 She put her left hand to the nail, and her right hand to the workman's hammer, and she struck Sisara, seeking in his head a place for the wound, and strongly piercing through his temples.

27 At her feet he fell: he fainted, and he died: he rolled before her feet, and he lay lifeless and wretched.

28 His mother looked out at a window, and howled: and she spoke from the dining room: Why is his chariot so long in coming back? Why are the feet of his horses so slow?

29 One that was wiser than the rest of his wives, returned this answer to her mother in law:

30 Perhaps he is now dividing the spoils, and the fairest of the women is chosen out for him: garments of divers colours are given to Sisara for his prey, and furniture of different kinds is heaped together to adorn the necks.

31 So let all thy enemies perish, O Lord: but let them that love thee shine, as the sun shineth in his rising. And the land rested for forty years.

DEBORAH: THE ORIGINAL WOMAN OF DESTINY

DISCUSSION QUESTIONS

1. Deborah was a judge, political leader, teacher, spiritual guide, and prophetess. Which of those roles impress you the most? Name some women who hold these positions today (other than prophetess). Do they reflect any of Deborah's qualities?
2. How do you feel about women taking on leadership positions in all walks of life? Do you consider yourself a leader in your own life?
3. Deborah was called to serve the people during a time of crisis. Have you ever been asked to step up in an emergency or other critical situation? What did you learn about yourself from that experience?
4. Deborah was an extremely confident leader in a culture dominated by men and did not shy away from celebrating her status or military victory. Are you comfortable with those aspects of her personality?
5. Which episode from Deborah's life can you relate to the most? Which can you least relate to?

**BOOKS ON BIBLICAL WOMEN RECOMMENDED BY MY
DESTINY CIRCLE:**

_____

_____

PILLAR I: INTELLIGENCE

〜〜〜

"Deborah's personality is a jewel with many facets: she expresses
her religion as a politician, a strategist, an adjudicator,
a poet, and, possibly, as a mother."

—WILLIAM E. PHIPPS, *Assertive Biblical Women*

A DESTINY WOMAN'S PRAYER FOR INTELLIGENCE

God, you alone created me and I am thankful. Today I pray for intelligence, wisdom, and guidance in the things of the Spirit and the intellect, which also comes from you. Keep my mind from wandering. Help me to obtain and retain knowledge. As you did for Deborah, give me the intelligence to know when and where to move, and with or without whom. I am thankful for that which I already know, but seek to learn more in order to expand my horizons, my outlook, and my ability to engage others in meaningful conversation. Dear God, I thank you in advance for what you're about to do IN me and through me. Amen.

Chapter Two

CALLED TO NEW THINGS

The first step in the journey to becoming a Woman of Destiny is to discover the place of transformation and greatness that awaits you. This requires the wisdom of listening and reflection and is fired by the determination to move ahead into a new season of life.

By definition, to be wise is to think and act sensibly by using the knowledge and experience you have collected over a lifetime. Part of being "sensible" is thinking and acting with awareness. A Woman of Destiny is determined, experienced, and filled with the knowledge that comes from living life with eyes, hearts, and hands wide open. These are the qualities that help you reach in new directions, make choices, and reevaluate your priorities.

Setting new goals requires honing in to your deepest motivations and passions and following through with a real-world plan for how to turn them into a new way of life. The choices you made on your way up as a younger woman may not be the ones you make as you work with your new goals—plotting out your next season will lead you into exciting new territory.

THE SEASON II EXERCISE

Deborah was a wife, an icon of leadership, and a warrior. She solved problems for everyone in her community, but when God gave her a job to do she had to zero in on her mission. She could have it all, but not all at once. This is an important lesson in the goal-setting stage of the journey.

> *To live is to choose. But to choose well, you must know who you are and what you stand for, where you want to go and why you want to get there.*
>
> —*Kofi Annan, former Secretary-General of the United Nations*

A recent event in my life is a good example of how much can be at stake when making decisions at this point in life. About a year ago I was offered the presidency of a fledgling seminary on the West Coast. After having served with a U.S. president and as the president of a twelve-thousand-member conference for leaders, many people enjoyed referring to me by the title "Madame President," and it carried over well beyond the conclusion of those positions. The seminary opportunity had all the earmarks of a great vocational move and would launch me into the highest level of academia, at least on the seminary level. But there was more to factor in than my vertical career track.

My eighth-grade son, attending the same school he had since nursery school and dealing with the entire array of a thirteen-year-old's love, friendship, and hormonal issues, did not want to move away. He needed stability and wanted to finish his graduation year with his friends. He wanted his mom by his side and became very emotional when he shared all this with me. It became clear to me that his need for stability at that moment in his life was more crucial than my need for a lofty title. I chose to turn down the seminary offer and stay out of the job search—not forever, but at least for a while.

The impact that that decision had on the peace of our household and my own peace of mind was phenomenal. If my child had been distraught over our move to another part of the country, part of me would have been troubled, too, and this surely would have affected my work and the well-being of our entire family. As Jesus said, "For what shall it profit a man, if he shall gain the whole world, and lose his own soul?" (Mark 8:36, KJV), and I would add and paraphrase "and lose her son?" When making decisions about new goals and strategies for achieving them, a Woman of Destiny must juggle many things, carefully look at all the angles, and ask, "What's the one thing that's most important right now?"

> *When making decisions about new goals and strategies for achieving them, a Woman of Destiny must juggle many things, carefully look at all the angles, and ask, "What's the one thing that's most important right now?"*

An exercise that I call "Season II" is the latest version of a technique I have developed over the years that is very helpful for zoning in on where you are now, working out your priorities, and clarifying what you want to do next. When you get clear on where you are right now, it is easier to believe that you can achieve a new role or set of goals because you've got confirmation that you did it all once before. It's all written down in black and white.

Writing down who you envision yourself to be *and* exactly what you need to get there makes this exercise a defining activity during this moment of transition. As you work through each column, your ideas become real, visible, and doable. You solidify how to bring forth all your skills and experience into a new role you may not have considered before. You gather up your passed-over dreams from the sidelines and set them firmly in their rightful place as signs of what your new season will look like.

Step 1. In the first column of the grid, marked "Me: Season I," list the roles you are living right now, including your job/career title, and identify yourself in terms of your interests. Maybe you are a teacher by profession and movie lover, League of Women Voters volunteer, reader, and devoted grandmother. Take an inventory of your skills and attributes, including those you may take for granted (speaking a second language, the ability to remain calm in a crisis, a warmth that puts people at ease, or upbeat energy that attracts and inspires). This is your status quo, you in Season I.

Bumper sticker spotted in Eugene, Oregon:
REMEMBER WHO YOU WANTED TO BE

Listing your roles and interests may sound simple, but it can be a transforming experience. One of my friends, whom I will call Mary, discovered an important issue about her priorities when working on this first column. Her list began with a few obvious roles, such as "wife," "friend," "animal lover," and "writer," but when she tried to put a label on what she considered her most important role, she had to really work to find the words. Finally, she came up with "self-motivated seeker" and "beholder of the world," two poetic-sounding roles that she defined for herself. She was astounded that there were no labels for the essence of who she was—a woman who continuously reads and studies to expand her psychological and spiritual awareness and who is deeply curious about nature and the world. Mary learned that she often allowed herself to downplay the significance of this role because her culture/society did not even have a name for it. That new insight gave her deeper respect for "what makes her tick" and made her realize that her deepest priority in life, to learn and grow and understand the universe, was a noble one, no matter how "fringe" it may appear to society.

As you reflect on this list, consider how much you did to achieve and develop each item. Are there roles or identities here that you never dreamed you would achieve when you were eighteen years old and standing at the threshold of your adult life? Give yourself credit for having become who you are right now. It is also important to write down roles that are not pleasant or life-enhancing, such as a job that is no longer fulfilling or a group/activity that you no longer enjoy but keep attending out of habit. Have you taken on too many committees, stayed in a town that you don't like, settled for a relationship that is not viable?

Step 2. In the middle column, "Me: Season II," list the roles that you desire for yourself. When you add up the skills and interests you have cultivated in the past three decades, what new role can they create for you? What talent did you set aside years ago? What interest or skill have you always wanted to pursue, but other responsibilities took you from this path? What truth have you discovered that you want to start living by? This is you in Season II, a committed, renewed, and passionate Woman of Destiny.

> *Discovering your new roles and goals is not an ego-driven exercise, but a process of unfolding parts of your life that you were always meant to develop.*

When I finally envisioned myself as a preacher who integrated more of my talents instead of confining myself to tradition, I gave myself the permission and enthusiasm to create entirely new productions that reached people I had never reached before. In one transition phase of my life, I described myself in "Me: Season II" as an actress and producer as well as a preacher, and the fruits of that goal became my first Wall Street lunchtime worship services. Defining that new role allowed me to celebrate my gifts as a performer and bring together the talent and resources to bring an hour of inspiration to the business world in downtown Manhattan. Although I had often felt the urge to bring my passion for performing and producing into my career, I did not envision it as an actual goal until I worked on this exercise. I needed to name it to claim it.

Discovering your new roles and goals is not an ego-driven exercise, but a process of unfolding parts of your life that you were always meant to develop. Some of our best work can only happen in our more mature years, after we have developed the experience, skills, and insights that will take us there. I believe that our strongest desires come from a divine place—that's what gives them extraordinary energy and fills us with a sense of purpose. By spending quality time reflecting on what brings you joy and meaning, you are working on one of the most important pieces of fulfilling your destiny.

Step 3. The third column, "Required to Reach Season II," is where you list the nuts and bolts of what it will take to achieve the roles and activities you listed in the center column. You may need more education or training, money or grants, a writing workshop, or simply more time in your schedule to devote to one specific goal. And you *will* need a mentor, or maybe two or three.

My friend Mary listed "research local groups and events" in this column as one of the tools for developing the new role she defined for herself in column two. She was excited about fulfilling that role, which she called being "a member of a like-minded community of intellectual/spiritual adventurers" and used the Internet as her primary guide to finding organizations, talks, and programs in her area. When she attended a lecture presented by a psychological society about forty miles away, for example, she sat next to a woman who became a dear friend and the first member of her new "like-minded community."

> *By spending quality time reflecting on what brings you joy and meaning, you are working on one of the most important pieces of fulfilling your destiny.*

Don't rush this exercise. Return to it several times so that you can allow your vision of where you want to be in Season II to simmer and percolate. The three-column outline printed here is a template to illustrate the process—copy it into a notebook so that you have plenty of room for crossing out goals in Season II that, after careful thought, become less important as others take on more significance.

The Season II Exercise in Three Steps

STEP 1. "Me: Season I": List your current roles in life according to your work, interests, and relationships, e.g., "high school math teacher," "gardener," "daughter."

STEP 2. "Me: Season II": List the roles that you desire and envision for yourself, e.g., "motivational speaker," "photographer," "master home project do-it-yourselfer."

STEP 3. "Required to Reach Season II":
List the actions you need to complete to develop the new role or roles listed in column two, e.g., "schedule a public talk at the local library," "find a mentor," "take a photography class at the YMCA," "attend a patio deck construction workshop at the local home store."

Season II Exercise

Me: Season I	Me: Season II	Required to Reach Season II

Women are often surprised by the information that comes to the surface with the Season II exercise. Clearly defining where you are now in column one may shed new light on a role that you want to nurture as your main goal in column two. This portrait of your status quo may also draw out frustrating realities that demand resolution. Bringing attention to long-held yet neglected dreams may ignite emotions that, if allowed to flow freely, bring refreshing release. The creativity and brainstorming you do in column three can bring a flood of ideas that actually result in new ideas for Season II. Be willing to embrace the challenges as well as the thrilling opportunities that greet you when you work on this exercise.

Reflections on the Season II Exercise

I learned that I don't want to rush into lots of new roles, but concentrate on making the existing roles that I *do* like better. Much, much better.

It was a relief to be encouraged not to rush this, but revisit. I will keep revisiting this exercise because it made me feel like I could have more control over my own life and could systematically work toward improvement.

—J.L., poet and college secretary

It was centering to take time to map out all the various roles in my life just now. I was able to see that there are some things

(continued)

---

in place to have a more balanced life, but that too often I'm reactive rather than calm and purposeful.

In "Me: Season II" I envisioned developing more creativity in how I do my job: some enacted and artful worship things for the Wednesday night services, possibly doing a trip to the Holy Land, taking steps to have more staff support at church, doing things to become more fit, calm, rested. This was helpful to envision a different way of being in the world, to step back and look at how things might be.

—A.S., Presbyterian minister

In "Me: Season I" I define myself as a job seeker, single, senior citizen, friend, confident, and in debt, among other things. In "Me: Season II" I envision myself happily married, thriving in my job, loving what I do and getting paid for it, financially independent, involved in community theater and reawakened by it, and several other roles.

As I reflect on those columns, the work-related statements pull on me. Being able to support myself and make a good living are key to achieving the life I desire. So much of my sense of identity comes through my work. Then, without work, who am I? So, as for the nuts and bolts—money, love, reaching out, getting involved, taking chances and risks, being open, having gratitude, doing my best—I am hopeful that someday I'll get there. I'll get it right. I'll finally know a sense of peace.

—R.R., laid-off personnel executive

Like Deborah the judge, we should approach this life-changing exercise with respect for the time that it takes to hear all arguments and moderate a fair process. Demand clarity and thoroughness. Take a recess when necessary and return to the assessment in a day or a week, allowing more information to make its way to the surface. I promise that it will be worth the effort.

TOOLS FOR TRANSITION

I have learned a lot about assessing my new priorities from my friend Pamela Palanque-North, one of the country's top experts on applied behavioral science, who teaches government organizations and Fortune 500 companies about managing transitions, cross-cultural mentoring, workplace diversity, and the dynamics of difference. The president of Palanque & Associates and professor of Organization Development at American University in Washington, D.C., Dr. Palanque-North shows leaders around the world how to collaborate and focus on the positive value of difference, engage in global teamwork, and deal with change.

In her early years of training at Yale, Pamela was an intern for a psychologist who was doing some of the first studies on the interactions between men and women. In that and other surroundings where some of the smartest people in the country came together, she saw how "a woman's voice disappeared" when men came into the room. While delving into the study of women in authority she had the keen awareness to realize her need for "getting some authority" in her own life. She learned, as we must do as Women of Destiny, that in assessing the resources that we have to bring to each season of our lives, we must listen to our own stories and experiences and not shut down when faced with messages that run counter to our goals.

> *When assessing the resources that we have to bring to each season of our lives, Women of Destiny must listen to our own stories and experiences and not shut down when faced with messages that run counter to our goals.*

I invited Pamela to speak at a conference for women in the ministry that I give every year, and she shared some of the practical wisdom about leadership and transition that she brings to CEOs and leaders of nations. Women in the church deal with the issue of transition every day, although it is often a silent "discussion." Stepping into roles that have traditionally been held by men, women clergy live out a cultural transition on many levels every day, and they have very few opportunities to share their unique concerns about the territory. Women who lead churches need an extra set of skills and advice on how to envision new goals for their congregations, and the pearls we received from Pamela extend to all women.

> *You are never too old to set another goal*
> *or to dream a new dream.*
>
> ﹏﹏
>
> —C. S. Lewis

Her first piece of advice was about **Modeling the Way**, literally being the model for others to follow. When you are in a leadership role, how integrated are you between what you say and what you do? When you're leading and thinking of leading, take a look at your ability to model the values, principles, and policies involved. Maybe you have a little work to do in one or two areas in order to be consistent with the mission. As a Woman of Destiny, I know that I lead the process of assessing my new goals and developing a strategy to put them into practice. At that level of "modeling," Pamela's first point speaks to my ability to take my transition seriously, to recognize that I am truly entering a phase of life that requires new expectations, new priorities, new road maps. I must lead this journey and walk my talk. With Deborah as a model, I can reflect on her unshakable self-assuredness. She did not know what sort of conflict would come before her from one hour to the next, but she was confident that she had the skills, experience, and divine guidance to support the work. That is the attitude I need to take toward myself.

The second leadership quality Pamela explained was about **Inspiring a Shared Vision**. The most visionary leaders create a situation in which others are brought in to make sure that no important perspective is missed while building and refining the new mission. As women in transition—whether it is a forced change due to the loss of income during a recession or a voluntary change to move forward—we are wise to allow others in on the process. And we must choose those allies carefully. "When I was still making life changes," Pamela said, "I got on the phone and called three to five of the women who have had the greatest impact on my life. Some have authority in the field I'm in or are personal coaches. I say, 'Give me an idea of where you see me.' I don't do that all by myself."

> *As women in transition, we are wise to allow others in on the process. And we must choose those allies carefully.*

Like Pamela, I value the insights that a select group of women in my life can always give me about my place in this moment. They have a fresh, objective perspective on where my path is leading me when I am too busy or distracted to see it myself. They bring their own experiences to bear on their perspective of my situation, and I am grateful to be able to benefit from that. Seek out your closest allies, friends, or relatives or others who will respect your mission of creating new goals in the second half of life. Ask them what your strengths and weaknesses are. A real friend will tell you the truth about the good and the bad, and that is the kind of person to invite into your process of transition.

Pamela's third piece of advice was about **Challenging the Process**. The women at our retreat conference faced many situations that tested their conflict-managing style. Pamela taught us that we have to be very skilled at understanding our conflict mode and develop a specific method for handling challenges. Challenging or managing a conflict not only requires tenacity, resilience, and vision, but the ability to step back from the situation and appraise the nature of the conflict. Few if any of us had thought about responding to a problem in any other way than our natural, first inclination, whatever that is for each individual. For many it was to be gentle and skirt around the issue without making too many waves. Acquiring a range of ways to deal with conflict, even the most minor ones that may come up in a church office, was a new idea.

To be most effective, Pam said, you've got to build a repertoire of approaches that range from being accommodating to aggressive, with a sophisticated mix of others in between. The secret is becoming comfortable with a variety of approaches such as compromise, collaboration, or setting up a competitive framework. Simply demanding your own way is rarely an option. "If the only tool you have is a hammer, then the whole world's a nail," she said. "You've got to know when to avoid, compromise, or accommodate to keep moving forward toward the goal. Each type of approach is appropriate in a certain context. You also have to have guts," she said.

If one advances confidently in the direction of his dreams, and endeavors to live the life which he had imagined, he will meet with a success unexpected in common hours.

—Henry David Thoreau

It takes courage and resilience to keep growing and blossoming, with your leadership becoming more evident to your congregation, when there are some in the church who are not ready to see a woman become confident at that level. Many women acknowledged that they had the skills to move the congregation forward but did not know how to confront and deal with stifling attitudes that held them back. Rather than backing down and becoming silent, that is the time to step up to higher ground, we learned. Face the attitudes directly and demand that everyone be clear about where they stand. We knew how to be flexible with different personalities in our families and parishes and we needed to learn how to apply our dynamic approaches to difficult issues that at first seem impossible to change. Challenge the process by engaging the issues, Pam said, so that it can bring about growth and positive change rather than wider divisions.

Managing conflict comes into play for Women of Destiny when we encounter resistance both within and without during the assessment process. Resolving to take on a new direction after becoming comfortable with one or two roles built up for decades may bring up strong reactions within and without. The requirements that you list in column three of the Season II exercise may look too costly or taxing on your time and energy. Your common sense may shout at you to quit dreaming and be sensible, but with an attitude that challenges the process, you may hear an even louder voice tell you that no challenge is too big or beloved goal too out of reach. By challenging the process, engaging in the arguments that pop up in your head, you open yourself to answers. You move ahead and expand your potential by being willing to let the resistance lead you to an expanded notion of what is possible.

Managing conflict comes into play for Women of Destiny when we encounter resistance both within and without during the assessment process.

MEET YOUR MENTOR

In addition to enlightening us about modeling our principles, finding motivational allies, engaging rather than avoiding the process when it gets tough, and listening to the heart, Pamela stressed the importance of mentors for women in transition. She credits an incredible mentor at Yale for introducing her to the field that became her passion and helping her forge her strengths. Finding a mentor is the follow-up to the Season II exercise—once you have crystallized your vision, actively seek out someone who has unique insights into that role and ask for her advice. Plan to talk to someone who is doing what you dream of doing.

If your goal is to share your expertise and experience by becoming a public speaker, spend some time observing professionals on public television, YouTube, and other Internet sites. When you find one who resonates strongly with you, write her a letter. "Tell her why you selected her," Pam advised, "and why you think she is the most important source to have access to in order to redo your life." Be bold, no matter how prominent that person may be. You are carving out a new life and have every right to aim for the top to get advice and inspiration.

Another way to choose a potential member to whom you can write a letter is to contact people in your network who may have connections in that area. Make use of the business and social connections you have developed over the years by picking up the phone and asking, "Do you know any successful public speakers or anyone who trains them?" Look at your network, do some mapping, and make the calls. "You want to do some work to find someone who will help you make a change in your life," Pam said. "You've got to step up. They can do correspondence with you. You may also want to get someone who is closer to you in life. There is someone right next to you who could be a very helpful mentor. I believe people need exposure to new people and new ideas."

Mentors have been crucial in every major step of my life. When I was preparing for my White House fellowship interviews during the Clinton administration, I was blessed to meet one of the most sought-after coaches for high-profile women in the world. During a conversation with Dr. Arthur Caliandro, pastor of Marble Collegiate Church in New York City, I mentioned the fellowship and he said, "You want to go to the White House? A lady at my church can help you." There are no coincidences— I believe that that pastor's willingness to introduce me to Meg Armstrong, a woman who was to help me immensely, was evidence of God's hand in my journey. When we are committed to fulfilling our dreams, doors open, people appear at the right time, and signs flash from every direction to tell us that we're in the right place at the right time.

> *There are no coincidences—when we are committed to fulfilling our dreams, doors open, people appear at the right time, and signs flash from every direction to tell us that we're in the right place at the right time.*

I learned that Meg Armstrong prepares prime ministers, diplomats, and business leaders for delivering speeches, presentations, and other events in one-on-one sessions. All of her clients come to her by referral only. During our meetings, Meg outlined all the questions the White House interviewers would ask. She was not only well-versed in the fellowship process but in what kind of look would be most appropriate for each specific occasion, from the interview to formal dinners. She instructed me on the length of my skirt, color of my suit, and what kind of earrings to wear. She told me I was not going to eat much during the dinners because I had to be ready to speak at any moment. I learned what to do with my napkin and how to time when I would stop chewing.

I loved every minute of Meg's tutoring—her coaching, molding and "no joking around" disciplined approach. This was the fellowship I had dreamed of, the presidency that I wanted to serve under, so I considered Meg's "business boot camp" the preparation to be a four-star general like Deborah and conquer my goal. I knew there were things I didn't know, so I focused on being a quick study.

I have always approached life with an adventurous, explorer's attitude and have been competitive with myself, eager to do more, see more, and be more than I was the year before. Most of all, the spirit of God has always operated within me, giving me the trust and confidence that the people and things I need will be provided and the willingness to open my arms to them when they arrive. When Dr. Arthur Caliandro told me about Meg Armstrong, I *knew* I had found my teacher/mentor for that stage of my sister's soul journey.

By the time Meg was finished with me, I had established a comfort zone in situations I had never even thought about before. When I walked through the door for my first interview, I knew I was already a White House fellow. Meg had gotten every scenario right—the entire process went just as she said it would, including my successful outcome.

Planning from the Heart

In all of her years training leaders to master the arts of managing change, conflict, difference, and transition, Meg learned that much of great leadership comes from the heart. A Woman of Destiny can decide what to become in the next season of life by learning what inspires her heart. For many, this will be a role that involves inspiring others. A life transition is fueled by inspired goals, such as the one my friend Gini Booth discovered when she turned fifty. After working for a nonprofit for many years, she learned about a literacy program in her community in Suffolk County on the eastern end of Long Island, and something clicked. She was amazed by the statistics that showed that illiteracy was a still a big issue in the late 1990s and fascinated by the way people could function very well in their jobs and families in spite of not being able to read or write. The shame that went along with illiteracy struck her deeply and she felt motivated to quit her job and work full-time for Literacy Suffolk. She has helped change people's lives there ever since.

Gini's new calling was loud and clear, and she believes that a woman's new role in a new season of life will reveal itself with the same kind of fervor. "When you find it, your belly is on fire and you go after it," she said. In 2006 she became the executive director of the organization and has expanded its reach into the community in creative ways, such as working with a local medical school to help students handle non-English-speaking patients through "health literacy."

For Gini, the key to finding your passion is getting to know yourself. When an issue absorbs you, she says, that is a good sign that you have uncovered your new destiny. "I keep moving on because things need to be done," Gini said. "Right now, that is trying to make people more literate, allow greater communication levels, and level the playing field." The fact that one in seven people in her county are illiterate due to their foreign language background or, even though born on Long Island, never learned to read or write, compels her to raise the awareness about their plight and of the services provided by Literacy Suffolk. She is convinced that the greatest barrier preventing the illiterate from getting help is shame over their lack of ability. "Remaining hostage to shame is eliminating generations of people who can be more productive for the country and for their families and themselves," she said. "That's pretty much how I look at things. I'm a spiritual woman, but I'm also very pragmatic." Gini is very intuitive as well, which I will discuss in Chapter 5.

> *For Gini, the key to finding your passion is getting to know yourself. When an issue absorbs you, she says, that is a good sign that you have uncovered your new destiny.*
>
> ⸎

Another woman in my life who made a transition based on a deep conviction is Reverend Sherri Arnold Graham of Fayetteville,

North Carolina. After working for several years as an investment industry executive, she felt "a passion, a stirring to be more connected to people," she said. She felt unfulfilled, as if she were holding out on that young version of herself who had left corporate America for a time to work with Legal Aid out of a strong call to "help hurting people." Years later, after building a successful career, she realized that she was being called to the ministry and quit her job. She set up her own business as a management consultant and enrolled in divinity school, which she completed in 2007, and then began pursuing a doctorate in transformative pastoral leadership. Now a Baptist minister, she spends most of her time running the foundation she launched that allows uninsured and underinsured women to have annual mammograms.

> *To every thing there is a season, and a time to every purpose under the heaven: A time to be born, and a time to die; a time to plant, and a time to pluck up that which is planted.*
>
> —*Ecclesiastes 3:1–2 (KJV)*

Reverend Graham believes that taking the time to reflect on your strengths and what you want your legacy to be are critical for defining your new roles as a Woman of Destiny. Contemplating those questions steered her into a new career of service and a new set of priorities. As a spiritual leader who switched from "investing in commodities to investing in souls" and head of a foundation that brings medical services to women who would not otherwise be able to receive them, Reverend Graham is convinced that she is fulfilling the purpose for which she was born. Connecting with people in such productive ways "helps reignite my passion," she said; "helps me know these are the gifts I believe I'm supposed to deposit in the earth."

Turning toward a new life chapter with a willingness to become whatever God needed her to be brought two transforming events to another woman of the church, Reverend Violet Fisher. After finishing seminary at age fifty, she adopted her four-month-old great nephew and became a mother for the first time. She had never been married, and when she got "this little child because he needed a mommy" she began a new domestic life that paralleled another major change in her path. Violet had recently left her dual career as a high school English teacher and part-time Pentecostal preacher to enroll in the seminary and rejoin the United Methodist Church, her earliest spiritual home. Soon afterward she was ordained in the church and received a pastorship in Pennsylvania.

Serving in a mainline church was a surprising outcome for a woman who had been preaching in the Pentecostal church since the age of sixteen. Like other women involved in the Pentecostal movement, which did not offer professional clergy positions, Violet had developed a teaching career. But nearing fifty, she felt a strong call to commit herself to preaching full-time and looked to the UMC, which had been ordaining women since the 1950s.

Violet's strong leadership skills elevated her to several responsible roles in the church, and four years after becoming ordained she was elected the first African-American woman bishop in the UMC's history. That role put her in charge of 800 churches and 1,500 clergy, making her a powerful voice in the church.

Recently retired, Reverend Fisher is still going strong in her late sixties by preaching throughout the world. She feels that her role as a mentor to future women church leaders is the greatest gift of this season of her life. "I feel like a spiritual mother," she said. "The Holy Spirit has birthed so many children through me. I feel that God has not finished with me yet, not even in my older years. We can still bring forth."

PATIENT ASSESSMENT: A GRADUAL YET GRAND JOURNEY TO SEASON II

The story of my friend Westina Matthews Shatteen shows how a Woman of Destiny can gradually transition into new roles that reflect her deepening priorities. After teaching for a few years, Westina went back to school to get a doctorate in education and began working for a nonprofit foundation in Chicago. That first job in grant-making led to a job at Merrill Lynch in New York, where she became a manager of its philanthropic programs. She moved up to become the director of that division and the first minority and first woman to be elected a trustee for the Merrill Lynch foundation. Among the programs she created was a scholarship program that gave children guaranteed college tuition if they graduated from high school. Her innovative ideas and strong performance eventually earned her the position of senior vice president of Merrill Lynch Bank USA.

> *You must be the change you wish to see in the world.*
>
> ∽⌒∿
>
> —*Mahatma Gandhi*

In 2002, Westina put her passion for sharing her experience into a symposium called "Black Women on Wall Street," in which panelists offered advice and support relevant to that unique group. Shortly after that Westina began giving talks in various venues about the faith that played such an important role in her success. Her theme revolved around the words of wisdom that her mother had given her many years earlier when she was starting her doctorate. Her mother gave her a gold chain necklace with a small glass pendant that contained a mustard seed. "Honey," she told Westina, "I don't have much to give you, but I want you to have this. Remember, so long as you have the faith of a single grain of mustard seed, all things are possible, if you only believe."

That necklace and her mother's words stayed with her as she rose from success to success, and it also inspired her to tell others about how her faith impacted her life. Her spiritual "Have a Little Faith" presentations gave her an opportunity to share that philosophy, and for six years, Dr. Shatteen, as she is known professionally, juggled the professions of a Wall Street banking executive, public speaker, and author, writing her first book in 2003. That title, *Have a Little Faith: The Faith of a Mustard Seed*, came with a hand-filled packet of mustard seeds, and was followed by two more books that she sells at her speaking engagements and on the Internet.

As she wrote her books and people began hearing her story, women pressed her to lead a spiritual retreat and offer guidance. Those requests, in addition to the desire she already had to share her spiritual message, gave her a new goal to shoot for. She did not feel prepared to be a spiritual leader, however, so she sought out a program that would train her for that new role. She knew who she wanted to be in Season II and went forward with a practical plan to gain the skills that would make it possible.

After enrolling in the Shalem Institute for Spiritual Formation, an organization that teaches "contemplative leadership," Westina told her husband that it was time for her to retire from Wall Street. He was her sounding board, an objective yet supportive ally whose opinion she respected. When he said she wasn't ready because she didn't have a plan, she made a firm commitment to work on her writing and developing a spiritual practice at Shalem.

In 2009, at the age of sixty, she felt that everything had come together with her new goals and she retired from Merrill Lynch after a stellar career. "I'm moving to the next season of my life," she told me during her summer of transition. "A whole life has been waiting for me." The six years of overlapped work in the corporate world and personal development as a writer, public speaker, and spiritual leader were moving her toward a new place.

After forming a strategy for the new roles she wanted to inhabit as a writer and spiritual guide and following through with the work and training required for them, Westina began living her new destiny. She is now an adjunct faculty member of General Theological Seminary's Center for Christian Spirituality in New York City, where she also provides spiritual guidance, and is writing another book.

Westina's method for assessing where she wanted to be fits in with the Season II exercise, but with an extra visual component. She felt compelled to start cutting out pictures and words to which she was drawn in magazines and place them in a little notebook. She taped the pieces lightly so that she could move them around and called the notebook her Dream Book. Each image represented an aspect of herself and her definition of an ideal life.

> *Whatever is true, whatever is noble, whatever is right, whatever is pure, whatever is lovely, whatever is admirable—if anything is excellent or praiseworthy—think about such things.*
>
> —*Philippians 4:8 (NIV)*

In another little notebook she began listing the qualities she envisioned for her life. This was a challenging task because "smart people tend to overthink" such things, she said. Westina wanted to get down to the essence of what her ideal life would involve, and this meant moving from a goal of "I want to make seven figures," for example, to the more broad truth that says, "I want all my needs to be supplied." Her list of criteria for her life included "creative," "filled with loving kindness," and "giving." Throughout the process she felt guided by the words of Paul: "Finally, brothers, whatever is true, whatever is noble, whatever is right, whatever is pure, whatever is lovely, whatever is admirable—if anything is excellent or praiseworthy—think about such things" (Philippians 4:8, NIV).

These two hands-on notebooks became tools at the heart of Westina's decision-making process. She could trust each item in her list of criteria for her ideal life because they had been put there after long, serious, and meditative consideration. She put that trust into action when she got ready to move from Chicago to the East Coast. "I had two job offers," she said, "and when I looked at my list, Merrill Lynch had everything on it that I was looking for, so I said yes and turned down the other offer. That decision changed the whole path of my life." Had she not worked out a clear list of what she wanted, she would not have been able to see how perfectly the Merrill Lynch job description matched her ideals. Running the company's charitable giving program would not have been on her radar. But all the work she put into her notebooks paid off in a career that drew on her talent and creativity. By the time she was ready to move on again, she could rely on her strategy for envisioning her future and was willing to take her time to be fully prepared for her new roles as a writer, speaker, and spiritual guide.

Whenever I look at my own journal and wonder if I am spending idle time by reflecting on my philosophy and ideals, I think of Westina. Her intelligent, straightforward approach to constructing the foundation of her life in her notebooks reminds me that this practice is not only important, but absolutely essential in order to become what we are called to become as Women of Destiny.

During these times of transition for the entire nation, when the economy is forcing many to make changes involuntarily, the Season II exercise and reflections that go with it can be profoundly helpful tools for entering a new phase of life. "I urge women to begin planning early for the transition and not wait for it to happen to them," Westina said. "There are a surprising number of men and women who are laid off in the financial industry and have no plan. There are others who had always been considering other things, so they were more prepared for change."

An Outline of Assessment

Like the laser-sharp intelligence that powered Deborah's work as a judge and leader, our best resources must come into play when we take stock of where we are and determine where we are going in the second half of life. Each segment of this three-part process is equally important:

- By clarifying our current roles, attributes, interests, and passions we learn what to build upon and gain new respect for the gifts we have to bring to the world.

- When we carefully listen to our desires we reenergize our goals or develop brand-new ones that will define our lives in the new season.
- The new roles and activities of the second half of life are achieved by plotting out a specific, real-life plan of action and finding a mentor who will introduce you to the new territory.

As Westina expressed in one of her poems, "A Woman Fully Grown," we move from the terra firma of our forties to "quiet strength in our fifties," the strength that allows us to reorient ourselves to new roles and master the work to fulfill them. The decades that lie behind us were rich with experience, learning, confidence-building, family-making, personal discovery, and opportunities to love that led us to this moment. It all comes together to draw us toward a new task whose time has come. Women of Destiny are mature and focused, ready to apply their intelligence to a strategy for change. Westina's verses say it beautifully: "We are smart. We are strong. We are bold. We are brave. We are triumphant. / We are women . . . fully grown."

CALLED TO NEW THINGS

DISCUSSION QUESTIONS

1. Did anyone tell you that you were particularly gifted or talented at something when you were a child? Did you pursue that talent?

2. What has surprised you so far as you work on the Season II exercise?

3. What do you resist the most about your list of new goals in the Season II exercise? How can you "challenge the process" and confront those anxieties in order to learn from them?

4. Describe a mentor who has been influential in your career or one of your interests. How did he or she come into your life?

5. Have you ever experienced a rush of "opening doors" or "coincidences" after you set your mind to a goal or project?

6. What is one skill or ability that you possess today that you did not possess twenty years ago? Ten years ago? Five?

BOOKS ON GOAL-MAKING AND MENTORS RECOMMENDED BY MY DESTINY CIRCLE:

_____

_____

_____

_____

_____

_____

CALLED TO NEW THINGS
√ **CHECKLIST**

____ Take an inventory of my strengths, roles, attributes and interests as a precursor to the Season II exercise. Ask for input from friends who will be honest and objective.

____ Set up the Season II exercise in a notebook. Do not complete the work in one sitting, but take time to reflect on each column, return to them, and journal the process.

____ Consult my network to find potential mentors.

____ Write a letter to a potential mentor, requesting an informational interview.

____ Take the necessary steps listed in the "Requirements" column of the Season II exercise and move toward my new roles and activities that define me in my new season.

Chapter Three

EMBRACING HARDSHIP AS GOLDEN OPPORTUNITY

A Woman of Destiny acknowledges the life lessons she has learned and knows that every experience, whether painful or joyous, is an opportunity for growth, awareness, and compassion. The nature of wisdom—the intelligence that Deborah brought to her roles as judge and leader—is to value the lessons that life has taught us and to act on that knowledge to create a better world.

The difficult times we live in call on us to dig deep for real strength. By facing our trials we tap in to living springs of power we never knew we had. Tough times can bring out our best so that we come out on the other side with even more strength, ready for whatever the next day or economic meltdown may bring. But no matter how much we've already been through, we can still use more guidance along the way. Wisdom is about gathering up more knowledge, more experience, and more advice from wherever it surfaces. Wisdom, like wine, improves with age. Every challenge in life has meaning and purpose.

> *Every experience, whether painful or joyous, is an opportunity for growth, awareness, and compassion.*

Deborah's wisdom as a judge included her ability to see the bigger picture when listening to the disputes people brought to her. Brilliant judges, like Moses who came before her and Solomon who came after, spun harmony out of the most complex disagreements. Time after time I have witnessed a difficult situation transform into an opportunity with more advantages than I ever envisioned in the original plan. Staying alert and keeping the essence of our goals in mind, we can ride through our difficulties with integrity and trust that all is working toward the best possible outcome.

THE GIFT OF GETTING OUT OF YOUR COMFORT ZONE

I have learned to move on when I feel that I have given everything I can. The discomfort comes from small signals that turn out to be important messages. Knowing when a season has run its course always reminds me of the wonderful story of Elijah, whom God had sent to live by a brook where his thirst was quenched and ravens came to bring him food every day. He got comfortable and lazy by that sweet water. But after a while God had new assignments for him and dried up the brook. Elijah had to move on. When my brook dries up, it is a sign that I am about to move into a new stage of my destiny. It is not my destiny to stay by a brook and get so fed and comfortable that I lose my edge, my creativity, and my motivation.

> *If there is no struggle, there is no progress.*
>
> —*Frederick Douglass*

Moving on may mean taking a long break in order to get refreshed so that you can return with new energy to a post that had begun to lose its luster. Listening to that discomfort and acting on it is the right thing to do because your actions always impact others. For example, about seven years into my career as pastor of Mariners' Temple Baptist Church in Manhattan's financial district, I felt burned out. As a single woman I had made the church my entire life. I had no boundaries and was all things for all people. My Wednesday noon "Lunch Hour of Power" services had become a downtown institution with great media coverage, but I reached a point where my brook ran dry. Out of the blue I got a call from a dean at Harvard inviting me to be part of its President's Administrative Fellows Program. It was suggested that I ask my congregation for a one-year sabbatical and move up to Boston to start the program in one month.

Asking for a year off with pay seemed like too much to ask. Who did I think I was? What if I got the sabbatical but my church let me go permanently? Could I just walk away from something I had worked so hard to build? After giving it serious thought, I realized that the opportunity was too important to turn it away. Leaving my comfort zone brought up fears and concerns, but deep down I knew it would be worth it.

To my surprise, my congregation was happy to give me a sabbatical. Word soon spread that I would be leaving for a year and colleagues from other churches called, shocked that I was leaving and worried for me. "If you leave for that long, you won't have a church!" they said. I said, "If I don't have *myself*, I won't have a church."

I spent a life-changing year at Harvard in a fellowship that gave me new skills and helped me envision new paths. The experience also helped others in a way that I had not imagined. When I returned to New York, many women and men asked me how I got my sabbatical. They needed a break, a change, and by modeling that option I opened a pathway for many clergywomen to reenergize their careers and get on a fresh track. I overcame my fears about losing my job in order to take advantage of a wonderful opportunity, and that leap of faith made the option possible for other women. You have to have the courage to break new ground because it's not all about you.

Another season in life happened when I returned. There was a White House Fellowship, marriage, and two babies. Learning to balance family and faith and putting in boundaries where they had not existed before now were a part of my life. When I knew that it was time to move on from my downtown church I took another leap and founded my own church in the Bronx. A new mom with two children under three, I needed a new move, not just for me but for the stabilizing of my new family. Offering the same type of inspirational, high-energy lunchtime services I had created downtown, our church grew steadily and reached out to the community with mentoring, career training, and sports and dance projects that empowered hundreds of people. Fifteen years and a lot of growth later, I knew again that it was time to move on. I could no longer ignore the pull that called me to break out of the box and weave together something new out of the experiences that had brought me that far.

> *We gain strength and courage and confidence by each experience in which we really stop to look fear in the face. . . . We must do that which we think we cannot.*
>
> —*Eleanor Roosevelt*

The church had become my family, and from the outside it looked like everything was perfect, a pastor who loved her church and a congregation who loved her. But inside, the call for more would not let me go. Being a woman leader in the church brings up challenging issues, no matter how smoothly church life seems to be running. Not until I made some untraditional moves did those concerns come to the surface in a more direct way and show me the resistance I probably would meet if I followed my instincts and started putting together a new way to preach. I got a glimpse of things to come in 2002 when I was elected the first woman president of the Hampton University Ministers' Conference, the largest gathering of African-American clergy in the world. Each year, the conference draws about ten thousand clergy from traditionally African-American denominations to the university in Virginia. Although most of my brothers and sisters in the conference were proud to see a woman take the helm for the first time, there were some who were critical of my role. In any field, a woman will be criticized from some corners for rising too quickly or moving into positions that more traditional folks cannot visualize them entering. It was important for me to face that in 2002 so that I could get used to the idea that there would always be resistance when I made an unconventional move.

After fifteen years in my Bronx church, I got that restless feeling again. I was busy, but I feared I was getting too comfortable by that beautiful singing brook of a church that had become my home. It was time to take another risk. I believe that if you stay too long in a place where you're comfortable, confronting fewer and fewer challenges, you either atrophy or lose what you built up. I had also lost five family and extended family members in the five years preceding this time. My spirit was tired, grieving, and slow to take action before I left for a sabbatical, and it could not recover when I came back. It took more and more energy to not only leave home each day, but also to walk up the stairs to my office. Worst of all, I really loved that congregation. They had been loyal, and for the first time in a long time I was starting to feel failure. I had no vision for beyond that point and remembered the wisdom in Proverbs 29:18, "Where there is no vision, the people perish." Without a vision I felt wilted, dried up, and perishing. I had to face the reality that my assignment was done. Prayerfully and thankfully, I left a female successor in place as I had done with my previous pastorate (a Destiny Woman prepares for her moves).

To realize a painful yet critical truth and act on it is to make a spiritually mature choice that I call a Destiny Decision. I had to decide to take action. For me, it was time to leave. I had to close some chapters and tie up loose ends so I could leave graciously and well. That is the only way a new season can begin in the best possible manner.

> *To realize a painful yet critical truth and act on it is to make a spiritually mature choice that I call a Destiny Decision.*

For a brief time before making that Destiny Decision I was confused—why should I feel restless when I have brought together a church that is doing so much good and lifting so many lives? Why didn't I feel moved to take the church in another direction instead of being called to leave?

Before I could meet the next stage of my destiny, I had to let go of some deep-set ideas about success. I told my friend who was a therapist that I no longer wanted to pastor, yet he pointed out that I kept allowing my name to be submitted to search committees at some major churches. (Therapy can often provide one with an objective, caring, confidential listener with whom you can air concerns that you cannot share with others. As a spiritual leader—including my role as the chaplain for the New York Police Department—I am at my best when I am as clear as possible, thanks to the help of a wise friend who draws from his expertise as a therapist during our conversations.) He gave me Barbara Brown Taylor's book *Leaving Church,* a memoir by a woman close to my age who had the same number of years in ministry as I did when she decided to leave the parish ministry. I could not put the book down. She wrote about "compassion fatigue," a phrase that leaped off the page because it expressed exactly how I felt. It was comforting to know that someone else had gone through what I was experiencing. I read the book in two days, but I was not quite ready to give up my search for a major pastorate at a major parish. As it turned out, my therapist friend was on the search committee at the renowned Riverside Church, and my name was on that list. I couldn't let go of the idea that I needed a "big-steeple church" on my resume to round out my almost thirty-year pastoral career, so I was really upset with him when he wouldn't talk about the progress of the search with me. He would not violate the confidentiality of the search committee, and I accused him of violating my need to discuss it.

> *Like Deborah the judge, I looked at all the facts*
> *and respected my inner call for change.*

It wasn't until I learned that I did not make the final round of applicants that it hit me that I really didn't want the position. But I also learned, as one of my clergy sisters shared, "man's rejection is God's protection." A block that had plagued me for months finally gave way and I withdrew my name from the other searches. The irony wasn't wasted on me as I prayed and thanked God for the job *rejection*, knowing that I was moving in the right direction, with His protection, toward my real passion. Thanking God for the freedom to be creative, I allowed new ideas to flow. Learning that challenges, failures, and rejections are actually blessings is a key stage in the development of a Woman of Destiny.

During that time I also remembered Deborah's clear thinking, the intelligence that allowed a judge to sort out all kinds of disputes from one hour to the next. Deborah was down to earth, able to communicate with all kinds of people, very confident in her intelligence, *and*, as a prophetess, a highly sensitive woman who was comfortable with her second type of intelligence, intuition. Deborah reminded me that my instincts had always led me in the right direction and that I should not doubt myself. The unease that had taken me out of Manhattan to build a new church in the Bronx was proof enough that I was on track. After making the first leap, I had received all the guidance I needed to build up a new congregation. What more evidence did I need? Like Deborah the judge, I looked at all the facts and respected my inner call for change.

> *Learning that challenges, failures, and rejections are actually blessings is a key stage in the development of a Woman of Destiny.*

Besides my new awareness that I did not need to look for a bigger church, other signs told me that it was time to move on and take the plunge into something completely new. Like most churches around the country, we had to tighten up our budget when the recession set in. Every two weeks we could cover all of the bills except my paycheck. It happened so many times that I had to laugh about it, but I also recognized it as a signal. When I had to start living off my savings, the wake-up call was loud and clear. I had had fourteen wonderful years at that church and it was time to go. The brook, or "source" of funds that had sustained me, had gone dry—literally! Leaving my comfort zone of the church that had become my new home would take me back to square one in so many ways, but I let my trust in the signs overcome my fears. As I told my congregation, *recession is not a time for depression*—when your brook dries up, what are you going to do next? I took a sabbatical, which I had set up in my contract. I saw my lost income as an opportunity to take stock and entertain my passions about my next step in life. God gave me guts through my paycheck.

> *God spoke to me and told me that this was not*
> *a punishment; it was an assignment.*

INSPIRATIONAL LIVES: ETIQUETTE IN AFFLICTION

Among the Women of Destiny who inspire me every day by their example of embracing hardship as golden opportunity is Reverend Sherri Arnold Graham, whom I mentioned in the previous chapter. She left the business world to act on her passion for the ministry, and in another amazing transition, she turned her role as a cancer survivor into a force for good in other women's lives.

Sherri was thirty-six and on top of her game in a corporate career when she was diagnosed with breast cancer. She had no known family history and things were going extremely well, when "boom, a diagnosis," she said. Her first response was to pray about it and share the news with her close friends. Some of them responded in a way that hurt at first, but led her to a better understanding of a biblical truth. "They shared some thoughts that I wouldn't recommend," she said, "telling me that I was sick because maybe I didn't pray enough." She thought of the gospel story in which the disciplines asked Jesus why a blind man got his affliction; like her friends, they thought sickness was a punishment: "Rabbi, who hath sinned, this man, or his parents, that he should be born blind? Jesus answered: Neither hath this man sinned, nor his parents, but that the works of God should be made manifest in him" (John 9:2–3, Douay).

When Sherri prayed about her condition, she felt inspired that something would be made manifest from her experience. "God spoke to me," she said, "and told me that this was not a punishment; it was an assignment." She knew that she would survive and in some way work on raising awareness about the disease. That conviction helped her get through her treatment and also to forgive her friends for lacking some "etiquette in affliction," as she called it, knowing that they meant well and that it's sometimes hard to say the right thing in a time of crisis.

Sherri believes that in all things, particularly the hardships, God wants us to trust him unconditionally and perhaps he might want to prove himself though our circumstances. Undergoing treatment wasn't easy, and she doesn't paint a rosy picture of it, but Sherri considers her cancer experience a life's journey that led to miraculous things. She was inspired to use a $10,000 bonus from work that she had put away for retirement to start a foundation to fund mammograms.

"It wasn't something I immediately said yes to," she said, "because I was guardedly thinking about the stereotypes of breast cancer." She told her sister that she didn't want to be a poster child for breast cancer awareness, but ultimately felt that she had been called to do the foundation. "I wanted to make a difference, raise awareness, provide free mammography for ladies who didn't have health insurance," she said. The first year her foundation made partnerships with two hospitals and organized seven mammogram outreaches. Sherri was ecstatic to be able to make a difference in women's lives and envisioned doing the same number of programs each year. But as it turned out, the work was just beginning.

Those first outreach programs gave Sherri access to hospital CEOs and pastors in charge of major funding enterprises, which raised her operating funds to $100,000 per year. The tenfold increase came from a Cancer Society grant and personal donations, and the foundation now provides extensive free health services. "The return on that investment has been phenomenal," Sherri said. "Lives have been saved, cancer has become detected early, and hospitals have agreed to provide free health care. I'm amazed at what God has done from my little seed."

Live strong is exactly what it says. It's one thing to live, but it's another thing to live strong, to attack the day and attack your life with a whole new attitude. This was a gift for me. I guess before the illness I just lived. Now, after the illness, I live strong.

—Lance Armstrong

Everyone at the Sherri Arnold Graham Foundation believes that God is their financier—people enjoy giving to the effort because they see the results. The women most in need are the project's number-one priority. "An uninsured status gives them a VIP status with this foundation," Sherri said. "They get the royal treatment because that's our mission."

Sherri's journey from cancer diagnosis to treatment, survival, and changing the world parallels that of Lance Armstrong, the world-renowned cyclist who launched a foundation just one year after his cancer diagnosis. Lance's outreach may be on a larger scale than Sherri's, but their commitment to turn hardship into opportunity is the same—and equally inspiring. Lance was twenty-five years old when he was diagnosed with advanced testicular cancer that had spread to his abdomen, lungs, and brain. While taking an active role in learning about the disease and getting aggressive treatment, he developed his "Live Strong" philosophy and began raising funds for his foundation. Less than three years later he was cancer-free and inspired cancer survivors around the world by winning his first Tour de France.

Lance used his fame to gather support for a foundation that has grown into a major source of cancer research and information. With seven Tour de France wins now under his belt, he is one of the world's most powerful examples of how a positive attitude and intelligent, passionate approach to a life crisis can turn a tragedy into a force for good. Cancer gave Lance a deeper appreciation for life and changed him from a self-absorbed (and to some, arrogant) athlete to a warm and generous human being. He considers cancer "a gift" because it taught him how to live.

Stories of transformation in the wake of Hurricane Katrina can also inspire us to view the challenging parts of our journey as golden opportunities. Katrina hit the gulf region on August 29, 2005, and was followed one month later by Hurricane Rita. The two storms wiped out nearly 20,000 businesses and damaged about 81,000 more. Among the small businesses that lost most of its customer base was Tina's Cajun Creations, a company that made cookbooks and other gift items that were sold in a few shops in the New Orleans tourist district. Rather than throw in the towel when the city turned into a ghost town, the owner, Tina Emenes, sought help from the Louisiana Small Business Development Center. She learned how to revamp her business model and market her products outside New Orleans by selling them on the Internet. The business development agency helped her get financing to redesign her packaging and expand her product line, and the results took her business beyond her wildest dreams.

Working out of the city she loves, Tina's sales are 80 percent higher than they were pre-Katrina. New Orleans is still in desperate need of help, but Tina's passion for rebuilding a business created jobs and showed the community that anything is possible.

Whether a calamity strikes your health, relationship, finances, or job, these stories reveal that there is an opportunity to not only recover, but to break new ground and become even more useful in the world on the other side of the pain. The lessons enrich us from within and ripple out in wondrous ways, as Reverend Violet Fisher learned through her health crisis. Violet, whom I introduced in Chapter 2, the woman who followed her heart to a full-time career in the ministry and found herself raising a newborn in the midst of that transition, is also a cancer survivor. Her journey brought more balance to her life, which she took into her work.

"The breast cancer experience really put me in touch with my humanness," she said. "I was so caught up in my spirituality, working in the church, and disconnected from my physical self because I didn't have major health problems. And this really grounded me." Violet came face to face with her mortality, which deepened her faith and made her keenly aware of the need for women in the church to take care of themselves and become a support system for each other. "Most of the women bishops in the United Methodist Church have had cancer," she said, "and we talk about it." Before retiring, she used her leadership platform to urge women to care for their bodies with the same reverence they showed for their spiritual and pastoral responsibilities. In her decades of church leadership, no one had heard Reverend Fisher speak about these things. "I talked to all the clergy about taking time for yourself, renewal leave, sabbatical leave, time with your family. All my priorities began to change."

Every difficulty carries a purpose: "To them that love God, all things work together unto good"

—Romans 8:28 (Douay)

I am grateful to know Violet, Sherri, and others who were courageous enough to overcome obstacles, even the most life-threatening, and then gift the world with the acts they were inspired to share. They constantly remind me that every difficulty carries a purpose: "to them that love God, *all* things work together unto good" (Romans 8:28, Douay).

THE MATURE BRAIN: READY FOR CHALLENGE AND GROWTH

As nature would have it, our bodies are more ready than ever to take on new challenges as we set out on journeys of growth and adventure when confronted with periods of transition. This is especially relevant for those women approaching retirement age—a transition that can involve the discovery of exciting new abilities. Studies have found that by the age of fifty, the left and right sides of the brain have become more integrated. This creates more harmony between our thoughts and feelings, which makes us "cool out," or be less fearful or anxious when confronting a challenging situation. Two structures in the brain called amygdalae become less active, which makes us less likely to respond with fear, anger, or hatred or to dwell on negative feelings. We are better wired to "think" with our hearts as well as our heads. We have developed a healthy balance between the two that creates a new dynamic—a new type of intelligence that comes at just the right time.

> *As our brains mature and evolve, so do our knowledge, our emotions, and our expressive abilities. In turn, what we do with those abilities affects the brain itself, forging the new connections and constellations needed for further psychological growth. This realization should embolden anyone entering the later phases of life.*
>
> —Dr. Gene Cohen, founder of the Center on Aging, Health & Humanities at George Washington University Medical Center

This enhanced intelligence and mellowed-out attitude helps us tackle the obstacles that may come our way as we move toward new goals in the second half of life. Gene Cohen, M.D., Ph.D., founder of the Center on Aging, Health & Humanities at George Washington University Medical Center, has done pioneering research on this subject that he explores in his book *The Mature Mind: The Positive Power of the Aging Brain.* "In short," he writes, "midlife is a time of new possibility." As we enter this transition period, he writes, we are well equipped for the journey:

> While changing our perspective, age also remodels our brains, leaving us better equipped to fulfill our own dreams. The most important difference between older brains and younger brains is also the easiest to

overlook: older brains have learned more than young ones. Throughout life, our brains encode thoughts and memories by forming new connections among neurons. The neurons themselves may lose some processing speed with age, but they become ever more richly intertwined.

Magnified tremendously, the brain of a mentally active fifty-year-old looks like a dense forest of interlocking branches, and this density reflects both deeper knowledge and better judgment. That's why age is such an advantage in fields like editing, law, medicine, coaching, and management. There is no substitute for acquired learning.

To reap the most benefits of the mature brain, Dr. Cohen recommends five practices to help boost the mind's power and clarity:

1. Exercise physically: many studies have linked exercise to better brainpower.
2. Exercise mentally: Just like a muscle, the brain grows stronger with use; if left idle, it gets "flabby." Engage in mind-stimulating activities like reading or studying a subject that appeals to you.
3. Develop mastery: People who learn to play a musical instrument, speak another language, sew, draw, or practice another skill stay healthier.
4. Select challenging leisure activities: The following pursuits ward off mental slowdown, from highest

impact to lowest: dancing, playing board games, playing musical instruments, doing crossword puzzles,
and reading.

5. Make strong social networks: "Countless studies"
   show that actively interacting with others enhances
   mental and physical health.

Knowing that our brain's best years are still ahead, we can
reach toward our new goals as Women of Destiny with even more
confidence. The powerful intelligence Deborah models for us
and that helps us manage life's challenges is more accessible in
this new season of life than ever before.

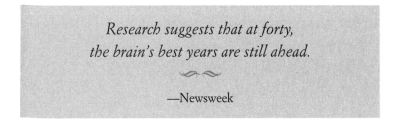

*Research suggests that at forty,
the brain's best years are still ahead.*

—Newsweek

For me, obstacles and hard times have been calls to action. I
listen to the urge to move on, do my homework about what direction ignites the most passion, and step onto the new path. The
first move is a risk, but there are wonders on the other side. When
the status quo no longer challenges you or a crisis shoves you out
of your comfort zone, make an intelligent evaluation of your best
options—and go for it.

1. Why do you think we grow more from struggle/challenges than positive events in our lives?
2. Describe an event that seemed disappointing at first, but that you later realized was a blessing in disguise.
3. Is there a conflict or nagging pattern in your life that, considered thoughtfully, may be viewed as a signal that something needs to change?
4. What were you taught about the maturing brain when you were in school?
5. What does it mean to "think with your heart"?
6. Are you more calm when faced with stress-making situations than you were ten or fifteen years ago? Have you noticed this change in anyone?

BOOKS ON HARDSHIP AS OPPORTUNITY RECOMMENDED
BY MY DESTINY CIRCLE:

_____

_____

_____

_____

_____

EMBRACING HARDSHIP AS GOLDEN OPPORTUNITY
√ CHECKLIST

___ Review the actions listed in the third column of the Season II exercise. List them on a separate page and rank them in order of difficulty. Remind yourself that each challenge holds the promise for rewards beyond those you have envisioned in your new roles and activities listed in column two.

___ To nurture my maturing brain, exercise regularly.

___ Exercise my brain regularly with engaging activities like reading.

___ Begin a skill-intensive practice, such as learning a language.

___ Once a week, go dancing, play a board game or musical instrument, do crossword puzzles, or read.

___ Attend a social event where I will interact with others.

MY PILLAR I CONTRACT WITH DESTINY

I am gifted with the intelligence, clarity, and enthusiasm to assess my strengths and talents and pursue an exciting new road map for the next chapter of my life. Challenges and obstacles do not slow me down but are priceless opportunities to grow. Every event in my life has meaning and purpose on my journey as a Woman of Destiny.

PILLAR II: SPIRITUALITY

We need to find God, and he cannot be found in noise and restlessness. God is the friend of silence.

—MOTHER TERESA

A DESTINY WOMAN'S PRAYER FOR SPIRITUAL GROWTH

Dear God, in your Word you indicate that Jesus grew in wisdom, stature, and grace and that He was also surrounded by people of faith from birth until the end of his life. If Jesus kept growing, then I want to keep growing, too. I want my SPIRIT to SOAR—in you. I understand that all that I am and ever hope to be I owe to thee. Please be my SGS, my Spiritual Growth System. Just as a voice comes over my GPS in my car and guides me toward the right path, I ask for your instructions—to keep me grounded in you, like the "tree planted by the rivers of water" (Psalm 1) where my Spirit is so deeply rooted in you that my soul grows big like Deborah's palm tree. I know I may bend when the hurricanes and storms of life come, but I will not break because I am in YOU.

Chapter Four

LIFTING UP YOUR SACRED SELF

One of Deborah's responsibilities as a judge ordained by God was to pray for her people. Reaching out to God with concerns, thoughts, questions, thank-yous, requests, and praise was in the job description. Deborah led a prayerful life and invites Women of Destiny to do the same.

Like Deborah's ability to allow divine wisdom to flow through her, we can nurture spiritual practices that open our hearts and minds to God. When a Woman of Destiny develops her sacred self, she connects to her true source of strength. The energy she devotes to her inner life is just as important as the energy she brings to the acts she does in the world. Building a spiritual life involves developing a prayer practice and carving out a time and place for reflection.

I was born into a family that practiced a prayerful life. We were an intergenerational household with grandparents, aunts, and my immediate family all around, and one of my earliest memories is of my grandmother kneeling down and teaching me the Lord's Prayer when I was about three years old. Every night I saw my father kneel down before he went to bed; he was a praying man. There was always prayer at the beginning of a meal and in the morning as we were sent off to school. Around the Thanksgiving table, every person went around and said thanks to God and read their favorite scripture. My home was not only a house of prayer but also a social center of the community; we had the minister, deacons, and elders to our house for dinner almost every Sunday. Blessed with thirteen godmothers, I was part of an extended church family we called the Inner Circle, a little Christian social club. We were a family that believed that no matter what crisis we were going through, we could always go to God. The spiritual life was part of my being; I formed a relationship with God very early on.

I know men and women who share a similar upbringing, but growing up in a Christian household and attending church is not the only path to a spiritual life. For many, the traditional church was never an option, and for those whose experience in one denomination or another left them skeptical, "organized religion" isn't their cup of tea. And even if someone does go to a traditional church, it may not be relevant enough. That is why I created the lunchtime services in New York and an unconventional

worship service at the Apollo Theater in Harlem. People ultimately want to know—how does God matter to my life? Forcing
a tradition upon someone is not the answer, but finding a way to
make spirituality a vital part of life is essential for every Woman
of Destiny.

> *God enters by a private door into every individual.*
>
> *—Ralph Waldo Emerson*

My college experience with an African-American church that
combined my intellectual curiosity and spiritual life gave me the
template for creating a balance between mind, body, and spirit.
Filled with students from Boston University, MIT, and Emerson
College, where I was getting a degree in mass communication,
the six-hundred-member church was full of smart young people
who came together to affirm, confirm, and celebrate their faith.
Sixty of us who sang in the eighty-voice choir eventually became
pastors, and other members went on to become doctors and Wall
Street whizzes—one is even an astronaut. Along with my very
early introduction into a prayerful life, my years at this church
formed my spiritual foundation. I realized that it is possible to
have the whole package, a stimulating life of both the mind and
the spirit, and that combination is at the heart of becoming a
Woman of Destiny.

I realized that it is possible to have the whole package, a stimulating life of both the mind and the spirit, and that combination is at the heart of becoming a Woman of Destiny.

WHAT IS PRAYER?

I believe that prayer is not only an action, but also part of who we are. The Genesis story tells us that God created man and woman and blew into our nostrils the very breath of life. From God's spirit came the human spirit. Because we are connected to our creator in this way, we naturally seek to get closer to God. For me, prayer is how we make that connection.

There is no single, specific way to pray. The style of prayer runs the gamut of reciting longish prayers like the Lord's Prayer to letting out an "Oh God!" I believe it is that simple—as Paul reminds us, God hears our "groaning" and delivers us (Acts 7:34). The practice of prayer is all about connecting.

My friend Mercedes Nesfield, a retired teacher, assistant principal, and New York City Board of Education administrator, comes to mind when I think of the call the inspiration to "pray without ceasing" (1 Thessalonians 5:17). At seventy-six, Mercedes has developed such a close relationship to God that she sees every moment as an opportunity to connect. When I called her on a December day to talk about her prayer life, she had just returned to her apartment from a walk while listening to her favorite singer on the iPod her son gave her for Christmas. She told me that she had had a beautiful day, running an errand on the streets of Manhattan in her tennis shoes. "I'm walking to the bank, healthy, happy, and listening to Barbra Streisand," she said. "You've got to stop and give God praise for that! How can I take that for granted? Ten blocks away, there are people in St. Luke's Hospital wishing they could do what I'm doing."

When you take the time to pray and develop a relationship with God, you come to know God's voice. You don't have to question whether or not it came from God. You learn how to dance as a team.

> *As soon as my feet hit the floor I thank*
> *God for this day.*

I try to live a life of prayer without ceasing; as soon as my feet hit the floor I thank God for this day. Before we start the car to go to school, my sons and I pray for protection. If they have an exam we'll pray that the knowledge they gained from their studying will come to them. Most of my prayers are prayers of thanksgiving, but I also pray a lot for the protection and health of teenage boys. There are very few moves I make without prayer.

Sometimes prayer is shared and sometimes it is a private

thing. The most important thing to remember about the practice of prayer is that we don't have to go through anyone to connect to God. Deborah did not pray for her people because they asked her to, but because they had separated themselves from God and did not pray on their own. I imagine her sitting beneath her tree, silently asking God to guide her as she listened to people's conflicts and considered the best way to resolve them. She was a model of the prayerful life and of putting God first, a woman who opened herself to divine wisdom in order to share it with her community.

Gathering with other people to worship is one thing, but most of the time praying should be a private matter shared with those closest to us or practiced alone. If you make time privately for God, God makes time privately for you. That is Jesus' advice on prayer, which he gives just before he recites the Lord's Prayer in Matthew 6. Jesus says that people who make a big deal out of praying in public are just doing it to get attention—"that they may be seen by men." The best way, he says, is to "enter thy chamber, and having shut the door, pray to thy Father in secret: and thy Father who seeth in secret will repay thee" (Matthew 6:6, Douay). To me, going into my chamber means going inside my heart, getting quiet, focusing on God, and making the connection. I don't have to be at home behind closed doors to be in my "chamber"; my chamber is here and now, behind my closed eyes or, even if that is not possible, simply my focus on God. Physician Larry Dossey, whose book *Healing Words* explores prayer and medicine, says the same thing about prayer technique, advising us to just "turn inward and turn upward."

> *If you make time privately for God,*
> *God makes time privately for you.*

More than a hundred scientific papers have been written about the effects of prayer on healing, and while some studies show that patients who were prayed over had better medical outcomes, others reveal that there was no significant difference. The "lab" results are inconclusive, but it may be that researchers have not yet figured out how to set up the perfect study for something as ethereal as prayer.

> *Prayer does not change God,*
> *but it changes him who prays.*
>
> —*Søren Kierkegaard*

I have been inspired by some of that research, but it doesn't really make any difference for me either way. The only test I trust is the one in my own prayer life and in the lives of family and friends whose experiences ring with the same truth of my own. When you experience God's response to prayer in your life, you *know.* God may answer in a way that you do not expect, but God answers.

PRAYER STORIES

There are times when you run into situations with all kinds of drama, when nothing runs smoothly no matter how well you planned. During one of those bumpy passages, I remember saying to God, "You have to show me everything. I need to know with wisdom what moves to make, when to make them, what questions to ask." After making that prayer, I woke up every morning at 4 a.m. and God gave me a "letter," a solution to one piece of the problem. The crisis lasted for three months, and I got through it because I got the information I needed from God in those early-morning answers to prayer.

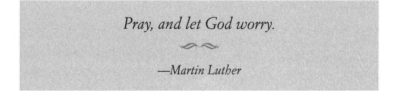

Pray, and let God worry.

—*Martin Luther*

Four a.m. seems to be an especially powerful time for me to connect to God. Recently, the Lord woke me up again at 4 a.m. and reminded me about a lease extension I needed. God told me who to talk to and what I should say, and when I followed up that day the lease extension was granted. That's what I call pointed answer to prayer, when you're pointed exactly in the direction you're supposed to go.

Another answer to prayer involved my year of leading the Hampton University Ministers' Conference. Two thousand women contacted me after I was named president and asked me to mentor them over the four years of my term. There was no way to mentor them individually, so I organized an event apart from the main conference in which the women could take a retreat and be nourished. Many of them had full-time jobs in addition to their pastoral work and lived in small towns or rural areas, so they were hungry for fellowship. Three hundred women attended the first conference, which we held in Fort Lauderdale, and afterward many prayers went out that the event would continue. In 2009 we held the sixth conference, now called the Women in Ministry International Summit. I didn't realize how great the need was. The yearly summit is an answer to many prayers, a safe place where women from around the world can connect to God and one another.

When the date of the main Hampton Ministers' Conference came near, my mother's health was failing and I struggled to decide whether to stay with her or attend the historic event. With my role as the first woman president of the conference, we knew we were ushering in a new era and had invited a slate of high-profile people like Carol Moseley Braun, America's first and only African-American woman senator; the late Dorothy Height, the famous civil rights activist and former president of the National Council of Negro Women; and Coretta Scott King, the widow of Dr. Martin Luther King, Jr. In spite of that, I was reluctant to leave my mother, who seemed near the end.

> *We work, we pull, we struggle, and we plan until we're utterly exhausted, but we have forgotten to plug in to the source of power. And that source of power is prayer.*
>
> —*Evelyn Christenson,*
> *author of* What Happens When Women Pray

I prayed over the situation and remembered the story about Hezekiah, who prayed to God when he was sick and about to die. God told him, "I have heard thy prayer, and I have seen thy tears: behold I will add to thy days fifteen years" (Isaiah 38:5, KJV). I asked God for just fifteen extra days of my mother's life so that I could go to the conference and return with enough time left to properly say good-bye to her. God answered that prayer—and then some. I got six months. Mom was hovering between life and death when I left for Virginia, but when I got back she revived and I had wonderful quality time to spend with her and make closure.

Years later, when Coretta Scott King got sick, I prayed that I would be able to be one of her pastors during her time of illness. She called herself my "other mother" and had really been like my second mother, and I thought my heart would break if I could not be at her side. Lo and behold, after making that prayer I got a call from one of her children, who said, "Mother would like you to come down." Spending time alone with Mrs. King, praying and making her laugh, as I loved to do, and giving her comfort before she died were special, private moments that only God could have ordained.

> *"There's an expression from Jeremiah, 'a burning fire shut up in my bones,'" she said, "and that's how it felt. I knew it was going to be all right."*

Mercedes Nesfield has the most creative prayer practice I know. After she became the assistant to the president of the Board of Education, she had to research and write up detailed reports that seemed overwhelming at first. To avoid getting tied up in knots, she wanted to pray for clarity and assurance, but she couldn't do it in sight of everyone. She came up with a routine of going into the ladies' room where, if she wasn't alone, she would sing to express her prayer. "I would be singing or humming a song of faith and friends would say, 'You're happy today, that's a nice song,' but I was actually praying."

Mercedes continued to move up at the Board of Education, and she believes that without a prayer practice she would not have been as successful in each of her stressful positions. When she was the director of the board's Office of Equal Opportunity, she was tasked with placing more minority teachers in schools that had become entrenched in a non-diversity mind-set. During meetings with schools she presented the facts about their ratio of minorities to non-minorities and introduced a plan of action, and usually met with a lot of resistance. "They didn't want anything else because what they had was working," she said. At times like that she silently prayed for God to see her through, and the response was always the same—a rush of energy that instantly calmed her. "There's an expression from Jeremiah, 'a burning fire shut up in my bones,'" she said, "and that's how it felt. I knew it was going to be all right."

Mercedes asks for that calm and confidence every time she gets up to speak, which she is often called to do as the president of the congregation at Canaan Baptist Church of Christ in Harlem. "I always say, 'Lord, speak through me, use my mind, my body, and my tongue. God, I know you're standing with me, give me the words.' Nothing long, nothing deep, just 'God, I know you're with me, speak for me.'"

Like Mercedes, I try to live a life of prayer without ceasing; as soon as my feet hit the floor I thank God for this day. By turning inward while we go through all the motions of our busy lives, we bring God into it all. And this is the key to developing your sacred self.

PUT GOD FIRST

Asking for God's presence in everyday situations like Mercedes described is an ideal way to begin living a prayerful life. It is not only about prayer, but about practicing the presence of God. Prayer opens the connection, and acknowledging God's presence shows that God is your priority. When you put God first you honor your sacred self, the part of you that doesn't think or rationalize but instead surrenders to God.

When I was a child we use to sing a song, "If you make one step, God will make two." That's what happened when I prayed for more time with my mother. God has much more in store than you imagine—we always think so small! And we usually do something first, then ask God to bless that action. It is much more efficient to confer with God first and open the connection so that God is your partner in everything. I believe that God says, "Where I guide I also provide. I'm going to give you the provision for this vision."

Connect with God first, pray silently, surrender to a loving attitude, and God will take care of the rest.

Putting God first is the most important step in developing a life that honors your sacred self. A Woman of Destiny who is balanced in this always asks for guidance and prays for a calm and clear mind, patience, compassion, strength, and the ability to approach every situation with love. Jesus tells us that when we attend to those qualities first, everything else will fall into place. "Seek ye first the kingdom of God, and his righteousness; and all these things shall be added unto you" (Matthew 6:33, KJV). I believe that this kingdom is a spiritual place, as Jesus says in John 18:36 KJV: "My kingdom is not of this world." If the kingdom is the sacred self we create when we are connected to God, and we put this before everything, we'll be on the right track.

When you get caught up wondering if something is too small or worldly to pray about, remember those words, *seek ye first the kingdom*. Connect with God first, pray silently, surrender to a loving attitude, and God will take care of the rest.

Putting God first has become part of my spiritual DNA. I can't make a move otherwise because God is my partner.

FIND YOUR STILL PLACE

Prayer is an inward practice, but it is also very helpful to find a place in the world that nurtures your spirituality. Find a quiet place, preferably one that is designed for contemplation, where you can be still at least once a week. This may be a church or temple, whether you're a believer in that faith or not. Spending a lunch hour in a quiet, holy place during your work week nurtures your soul. It helps bring balance because you are affirming that you are both a spiritual and earthly being. Sitting quietly, turning off your cell phone, letting your mind free itself from work and everything else is not asking too much. You deserve to let it all go for thirty minutes and relax. My grandmothers in the South used to say, "Sit down and settle your nerves."

Sitting in a quiet place where other people are nurturing their souls is deeply comforting. I learned that when I started my lunchtime services in downtown Manhattan. Word spread that we had created an uplifting, spiritual space in which no one would be judged or asked if she were a Christian or not. The service became especially important after the tragedy of September 11, 2001, when shell-shocked souls flooded through the doors looking for consolation. People were hysterical; they had seen people dropping out of buildings. They did not know what was on the other side of their shock and grief, but they had this church to come to. Their eyes were huge and teary and they walked without confidence, but after a half hour of loving community they left with more power in their steps. And they came back, grateful for a place that would help them get through the next few days and weeks.

That's what the scriptures call refuge in a time of trouble. That's what a faith place is. If I'm on Fifth Avenue and I feel I need to stop because the city's feeling too fast and eight million people are bumping into me, I'll go into St. Patrick's Cathedral and sit in a pew. It is like walking into another world, which it is.

You can also create a still place by reading an inspirational book. If you cannot get to a meditative place over your lunch hour once a week, reading a book that nurtures your soul will achieve the same thing. Getting into the habit of reading inspirational books before you go to sleep is a powerful practice, although it may take some discipline to turn off the TV and read instead. Everyone likes to unwind at the end of a long day by zoning out in front of the TV for an hour or so, but reading a book or listening to a tape that supports your spiritual development is better. Change your routine and put God first, lift up your sacred self, and bring balance to your spiritual and earthly nature.

> *We must learn to slow down and not run away*
> *from ourselves. Part of our multitasking must be*
> *setting aside time to focus on the inner life.*

REMEMBER YOUR OWN SABBATH

Part of my spiritual development calls for slowing down at regular times in order to achieve balance. In addition to finding a "still place" that brings a holy center to your work week, look for ways to integrate longer periods for rest and reflection in your schedule.

Whether you live in a city, suburb, or small town, you probably juggle work and many other commitments. Anywhere in America, life moves fast, and a spiritual journey demands just the opposite. We must learn to slow down and not run away from ourselves. Part of our multitasking must be setting aside time to focus on the inner life.

The best-case scenario is to take one day each week as your Sabbath, your time for reflection and spiritual nurturing. If that is not possible, devote a full day at least once a month to quiet contemplation and nurturing your stressed-out body and soul. This is the day you honor God by setting aside everything else. Stepping out of your routine allows you to see where you are more clearly and helps you put some pieces together that you are otherwise too distracted to handle.

You love the look of your shiny bathtub, but when was the last time you actually used it? On your day off, fill it with hot water and perfumed soap and lie in it for an hour, listening to tranquil music or just the silence. Relax and take an inventory of the activities and people who are nourishing you and those who are not. Some people are lifelong companions, but others are meant to come into our lives for only a season. What may have nourished you for that interval in your life is no longer supportive and may even be draining your energy. You do not have to figure out how to tell that person good-bye; pray for help, and the situation will take care of itself.

One of my friends spends several hours of her personal Sabbath days watching DVDs of inspirational speakers like Deepak Chopra, Caroline Myss, and Wayne Dyer, all while soaking her feet and giving herself a pedicure and manicure. No commercials, no interruptions, just pure inspiration and luxury! Even though she does two things at once, they are both geared to her soulful comfort. Pay attention to how restless you become when you settle down to read, write in your journal, or watch one of your favorite speakers when you have an entire day to yourself. We are so used to doing as much as possible in a day that it feels strange and even *wrong* to relax and do just one thing at a time. But that's the purpose of your personal Sabbath, to completely shift gears so that you can listen, absorb, rest, and recoup.

A regular practice that I have created that puts a piece of the Sabbath in every day is writing down the next day's to-do list before I go to sleep. This helps me relax and sleep well because I have attended to all my unfinished business. It also helps me create boundaries each day, because there is often not enough time in the day to finish everything I put on the list. I have gradually learned to cross out things that I know cannot be done on any given day and let them go. I prioritize for me and put boundaries on the day so that I can go home to attend to my family and my personal time and not take work with me. If I accomplish only half of what I wrote down for that day, I thank God for giving me the time and resources to do them.

A Woman of Destiny lives in spiritual balance by taking her daily bread—a doable workday—not a week's worth of activity crammed into nine or ten hours.

A Woman of Destiny lives in spiritual balance by taking her daily bread—a doable workday—not a week's worth of activity crammed into nine or ten hours. She does her best within her allotted work time and gets enough sleep so that she can bring the same devoted attention to the next day's work.

Taking time to refresh the spirit is not a luxury but a necessity. Work is important, but to everything there is a season. A time to keep silence, a time to heal, a time to dance and a time of peace (Ecclesiastes 3). These are the times that make up your personal Sabbath.

THE POWER OF TRUSTING

In my work as a chaplain for the New York City Police Department, I often do my counseling in bars. That's where some of the men and women on the force feel most comfortable talking about their spiritual concerns because they don't want anyone to know we're having that conversation. I dress casually and we hide out in plain sight. They consider me their spiritual coach, someone who is willing to meet them when and where it's convenient and keep it confidential. I call it "Church-to-Go."

> *Even when it looks impossible, when the enemy has worn you down with his iron chariots, your trust in God assures you that you can still conquer anything.*

My work as a "spiritual coach" for the NYPD and others involves trust. They trust that I will take them seriously, not judge them, and that I will speak from a spiritual place. I rely on my own spiritual coaches for the same thing. When I am about to take on a new project that I have not done before, I call on older fathers and mothers in the faith who have already walked that walk. Someone who has the wisdom and skill to enlighten me about a step on my path is a gift, and I follow their advice. I do the same for pastors who are walking onto paths I have already tread. We are a supportive community based on trust.

When God called on Deborah to lead ten thousand warriors into battle and told her that she would be successful, she never had a millisecond of doubt. All the odds were against them, and even her right-hand man, the famous general Barak, refused to go on the mission unless Deborah came along. Barak didn't put much trust in God in that moment, and Deborah prophesied that he would regret it by not being the one to slay the enemy, Sisera. Her prophecy came true when Jael killed the general in her tent. The second part of Deborah's prophecy also came true when the Canaanites retreated and the tribes of Israel no longer had to fear their nine hundred chariots.

A Woman of Destiny trusts that God intervenes in her battles. Part of this journey is learning to believe, without a doubt, that you can call upon divine help and trust in it. Even when it looks impossible, when the enemy has worn you down with his iron chariots, your trust in God assures you that you can still conquer anything. Deborah's Song in Judges 5 begins with praise to God—put God first, and the rest will work out.

Trust in the presence of God increases as you continue on your path. Each spiritual practice described in this chapter is connected and builds deeper trust, creating a circular journey:

1. Putting God first makes you prayerful
2. Prayer strengthens your connection with God

3. Connecting to God makes you aware of God's answer to prayer

4. Answered prayer makes you trust that God is working in your life

5. Trusting God, you put God first

6. Putting God first makes you prayerful . . .

If prayer is brand new to you and you have no idea how to start, here are my four recommendations: First, find a faith community in which your spirit can soar. The human soul is constantly seeking a "space for grace," a place away from the hustle and bustle of life. Stop into a faith place or go online and find a virtual prayer community. You may find a church or similar organization or a spiritual retreat center that offers special opportunities for developing your prayer life.

Next, just stop. Set aside a time and place once a day to close your eyes and turn inward. Even God stopped after six days of creation. Prayer is simply communion with the Creator, so as you sit, silently say "God" or "I thank you, my Creator" as you inhale, and the same as you breathe out, until the repetition causes the soul to meet the holy. The most convenient place for this may be in bed before you go to sleep—sit up, relax, and repeat that simple word or phrase. Spend five minutes a day on this for a full week and then gradually increase the time. As you allow yourself more time for a longer prayer, copy one of the prayers from this book onto an index card and repeat it throughout the day until it becomes your prayer with God.

Third, visit a place that makes you smile and brings you joy. I have a favorite spot in the city near the water that I call my soul's hideaway. As I watch the waves, my heart and God's heart connect. I make a list of all the things I am thankful for and offer that thanks to God (a prayer of thanksgiving) and then I make a list of things I desire or need and offer them to God (a prayer of supplication). Just twenty minutes or a half hour in this special place, thanking and communing with God, brings essential balance to my life.

Finally, ask someone with a strong prayer life to be your spiritual coach for a season. Tell him or her that you would like to learn to pray or enrich your current practice.

Becoming a Woman of Destiny is a spiritual journey that intensifies by the day, week, and year. Your sacred self becomes an equal player in the work you set out to do in your new season, creating opportunities and experiences that never existed before. To accompany all the days of your journey, I offer you the Woman of Destiny's Prayer. Like Deborah's ancient verses, it is both a song to celebrate your unique life and a focus for contemplation of your sacred self.

LIFTING UP YOUR SACRED SELF

DISCUSSION QUESTIONS

---

1. When did you first learn about God?
2. What have been the most significant spiritual experiences of your life?

3. Have you ever received an answer to prayer (that you know of)?

4. How would you feel if someone asked you to pray for them?

5. What is your most highly developed spiritual quality?

6. Imagine yourself devoting an entire day to your personal Sabbath, twenty-four hours set aside for your spiritual nourishment. Do you foresee any challenges in putting this into your weekly or monthly schedule?

7. Would you benefit from a spiritual coach? If you wanted to seek one out, what qualifications would you require him or her to have?

BOOKS ON PRAYER AND SACRED PRACTICE RECOMMENDED BY MY DESTINY CIRCLE:

_____

_____

_____

_____

_____

LIFTING UP YOUR SACRED SELF
√ **CHECKLIST**

___ Spend one lunch hour every week sitting quietly in a sacred/meditative space.

___ As often as possible, stop and silently remember my connection to God.

___ Before starting any activity, silently pray for God's help.

___ Silently thank God for every kindness and act of love that comes my way, every opportunity to see nature, every piece of work entrusted to me, and every opportunity to be kind and loving.

___ Ask friends for recommendations and/or browse the bookstore or library for inspirational books, CDs, and DVDs.

___ Devote one day per week or at least one day per month to a personal Sabbath, focusing on activities that nourish my soul. Mark the date in my calendar.

Chapter Five

THE GIFT OF INTUITION

Deborah served a sacred role as prophetess, a clear voice for God's messages. Today, some would equate that with the realm of psychics and mediums, but to me, the most useful connection between Deborah the prophetess and twenty-first-century women is our God-given intuition.

Intuition, the power of knowing something directly instead of going through the process of rational thought, is a natural type of intelligence and part of our spiritual makeup. It is that confident, immediate feeling of knowing something in your "gut" or sensing the nagging warning in the back of your mind.

Deborah never doubted God's voice. She acted immediately on the messages she received, and this is the perfect model for how we should respond to our intuition. By becoming more comfortable with your particular way of tuning in to your intuition, you can learn to trust it more often. Every successful action based on guidance from intuition will give you more confidence in relying on this powerful tool. As a natural facility that we are all born with, intuition is another type of human knowing that can uncover answers to questions that come up along the journey to becoming a Woman of Destiny.

A Spiritual Definition

As a woman of the church, I equate intuition with the Holy Spirit. I doubt, however, that you will find many churches dedicated to helping parishioners develop this gift, and I think we've made a mistake in not honoring it. It may be that intuition is associated with speaking in tongues and other acts celebrated in Pentecostal churches, actions that make other churchgoers uncomfortable. But I have no difficulty embracing intuition as a natural part of my makeup, one of the tools—along with my intellect, emotions, and five senses—that God created to help us relate to each other and receive divine guidance.

> *In 95 percent of high-pressured situations, decision makers rely on their intuition rather than a "normal" thinking process.*

Rather than ignore intuition's quiet messages, we should listen carefully and be grateful for them. We all carry a piece of the prophetess in us. Jesus said that after he left this earth he would send the Holy Spirit as a counselor and Spirit of truth, a holy presence that "will guide you into all truth" and "shew you things to come" (John 16:13, KJV). The messages we receive from our intuition are the Holy Spirit's nudging, and by listening to that still, small voice we incorporate Deborah's prophetic aspect.

Acknowledging intuition as a natural gift is the first step in making it work for you. Just opening yourself to the possibility makes you more receptive. Having an open and receptive attitude reminds me of the story of another prophet, Isaiah, who had a theophanic experience, or vision of God. But it didn't stop at that; in Isaiah 6 we read that God was getting him ready for his call. An angel touched Isaiah's lips with a hot coal in order to cleanse him from guilt and other blocks that get in the way. Isaiah was then able to hear God's request for someone to take a message to Isaiah's people. God asked Isaiah, "Whom shall I send, and who will go for us?" and Isaiah said, "Here am I! Send me!" (Isaiah 6:8, KJV). It wasn't that God hadn't been speaking all along, but that Isaiah finally got in a posture to hear. He had to get in the right frame of mind, receptive and open, to be ready to hear God. When you get to that moment, that's what the world calls intuition. Accept intuition as a fact of life and you're more than halfway there.

Rather than ignore intuition's quiet messages, we should listen carefully and be grateful for them. Intuition is real. We all carry a piece of the prophetess in us.

THE SCIENCE OF INTUITION

Psychologists and other scientists who study intuition have come up with some amazing facts about this aspect of our lives. Studies show that in about 95 percent of high-pressured situations, decision makers rely on their intuition rather than a "normal" thinking process. They take advantage of the mysterious messaging that goes on every day to alert us to important information. One theory about intuitive "knowing" explains it as a moment in which we get in touch with information that we stored away and forgot about. Other theories claim that there is more to it than that, and there is some interesting science to back them up.

Trust your hunches. They're usually based on facts filed away just below the conscious level.

—*Dr. Joyce Brothers*

I was fascinated to learn about studies that prove that intuition—knowing and responding to information without using our five senses—is wired into human beings. In experiments in which people were hooked up to sensors that measured their heart rate and other changes in the body, the participants were shown randomly selected photographs containing either emotionally provocative or calm images. The scientists found that the autonomic nervous system responded to the dramatic pictures four to seven seconds *before* an emotionally charged photograph was shown. The body did not respond to upcoming calm photos. One study went further to show that the heart actually responded faster than the brain a few seconds before a traumatic-looking picture came up. The heart, it seems, has a mind, too.

If the latest scientific studies show that our bodies pick up information about something just ahead that may put us in harm's way and alert us about it, maybe there will be future studies about other types of intuitive messages. Scientists might even get a handle on the type we call mother's intuition. I know all about that, as many women do, because one of my most powerful experiences with intuition concerned my son, Sam.

A Mother's Hunches

During the presidential campaign of 2008, I flew to the Democratic convention in Denver the Saturday before the events were to begin. Then-Senator Barack Obama was scheduled to give his nomination acceptance speech on Thursday night, and even though I had been working on Senator Hillary Rodham Clinton's campaign, we had all made the decision that we were going to be on the same team, of course. It was a historic time and excitement over the convention had been building to a frenzy. Even from the outside, the giant Invesco Field stadium at the foot of the Rocky Mountains looked like a place that could change history. It was going to be an amazing week. But as soon as I landed in Denver something inside me said I had to go home.

> *As soon as I landed in Denver something inside me said I had to go home.*

Everywhere I went people talked about how they couldn't wait to see this man, the first black nominee, make his speech in the stadium. I just kept feeling like I should hop in a cab and get on the next flight back to New York. Maybe something's going to happen security-wise, I thought, and Spirit is warning me in advance to get away. There was a lot of talk those days about Obama's people fearing for his life. Then I started rationalizing my nagging feeling, figuring that some part of me thought it would be better to experience the event with my sons. The feeling would not go away, so on Monday I went to the front desk at the hotel and asked if I could get a refund for my package stay if I left early. No, and it would cost me another $150 to change my ticket. I fought my hunches and made a compromise, cutting the week short by re-booking my flight for Wednesday night. Over those three days I saw, spoke to, and kissed everybody I needed to see and every night was wonderful. But I knew I was not going to hear Barack Obama.

On Wednesday night I took the red-eye to New York and arrived at 6:30 the next morning. The first message on my cell phone was from Hillary's people, who said that the senator wanted me to sit with her at the stadium that night. I thought about getting on another plane and heading back, but when I returned the call I learned that there was no way I could make it. Anyone planning to attend had to go through security several hours early, so it was too late. Shoot, I thought, the one night I could sit with Hillary and be her guest at this historic event.

The second message on my phone was from the management of the Manhattan apartment building I was soon to move into. They had called my bank to check on my funds for the deposit I was about to pay, and the account only showed $700. The decimal point was a bit off, so I called the bank to tell them they had made an error and that I was coming in with my deposit receipt. I went to the bank as soon as it opened, showed them the receipt, got that decimal point moved over a couple of spaces, and sorted it all out with the apartment management. If I had not been there, management probably would have torn up my paperwork before I even had a chance to move in.

The third call on my cell came from my office, which relayed the message that my son's New Jersey boarding school infirmary wanted me to call right away. Sam had passed out on the football field and the doctor had found some heart irregularities. The week before two players had passed out in New Jersey and died on the football field, so they weren't taking any chances. The doctor told me they would take Sam to the emergency room and that he had to get a heart monitor before the school would allow him back on the team.

> *Intuition will tell the thinking mind*
> *where to think next.*
>
> —*Jonas Salk, developer of the polio vaccine*

As soon as I got off the phone I called Sam's pediatrician, who was miraculously at her desk the day before Labor Day. She was able to make an appointment for Sam with a pediatric cardiologist the next day. I got in my car, called my husband to let him know what was going on, and was soon speeding down the New Jersey Turnpike. Not long afterward, Sam and I were home, settled in to watch the convention.

> *Don't let the noise of others' opinions drown your*
> *own inner voice. And most important, have the*
> *courage to follow your heart and intuition; they*
> *somehow already know what you truly want to*
> *become. Everything else is secondary.*
>
> —*Steve Jobs, cofounder and CEO of Apple*

What if I had been in that stadium in Denver and gotten that call? I would have been a basket case, my husband would not have been able to get Sam to a cardiologist because he doesn't drive, and my child would have been in some ER by himself on Labor Day weekend. I said, "God, thank you. I thought the bank was enough of a problem to run home to, but thank you for making me get back for my son." The pull to go home was the strongest intuitive message I had felt in a long time. No matter what the hundreds of my fellow convention goers were saying, I knew what I had to do. I had to go back to New York.

Another unforgettable hunch came to me decades ago when I was on a trip to Spain. My college roommate and I had registered for the trip, for which we would get college credit, but at the time my dad was sick and in and out of the hospital. I called home every day, and there was something in my mother's voice that pressed me to go home. She wasn't trying to alarm me, but I heard another message between her words. At seventeen years old, I negotiated the details of going home early, including paying the fee to exchange my return ticket and arranging with the tour leader to finish my work at home. It was a hassle and it broke my heart to turn around and leave that country after working so hard to make the trip, but I knew I had to go. The voice was so strong inside me that I could not ignore it. When I got home, it was close to Dad's time. He had gone back into the hospital and would not come home again. I was able to help my mother and spend some time with my dad during his last days.

Personal Encounters with "Knowing"

Reverend Sherri Arnold Graham, the friend I mentioned earlier, credits her intuition for guiding her into her new role with her cancer foundation. She calls intuition "a thread in the fiber of our lives that helps guide us to the purposes for which we've been created." Whether leading her down a new path or ushering her away from danger, intuition has been a factor in Sherri's remarkable and varied life. She views it as a synergy of both human and divine aspects, an experience with "divine inclinations" that she calls the moving of the Holy Spirit in her life. Leaving the corporate world and taking a new direction after surviving cancer were not things she had planned or intended, and at times she tried to move against these changes. Her intuition pointed her in all the right directions to start her foundation, but seeing the divine aspect of those messages in her and others' lives makes the biggest impression on her. Watching the Holy Spirit move people to do things that they would not think of doing themselves, and seeing how much good those actions bring to the world are huge confirmations that God is at work, she says. "There are a lot of voices out there," she told me, "and I love to know when we've heard from God because there's ultimately confirmation."

There is no way that one created in the very image of God will ever be totally disconnected from God. It's a matter of how we tune in. Taking the time to do it and surrounding ourselves with those who are also comfortable with this gift will bring our intuitive intelligence to the forefront.

Everyone who knows my friend Gini Booth is aware of her intuitive gifts. "A friend said I have an extra set of eyes," she said. A few of those friends feel privileged to spend a few hours at her home in Sag Harbor from time to time. She has a wonderful enclosed porch, a bright and airy little place with fifteen windows and delicate white sheer curtains where we sit and talk with a glass of wine and call it sittin' and sippin'. It's one of those places where we feel safe enough to share our dreams with each other and they don't sound crazy, but doable. Gini zeros in and tells me what I already have, what is waiting out there in the future for me. She has that kind of sense; like Deborah, she speaks from a much bigger place. When she talks to me it's about what I am going to do when I'm there instead of what I'm hoping and wishing for. "No, this one you already have," she'll say, and she's always right.

"You will survive," the voice said. "You will do fine, but it's going to be the biggest challenge of your life."

Gini has heard and closely followed her intuition since she was a young girl. Her family believes that she has always had a special gift. "I'm a light-skinned African-American woman with blue eyes and blond hair with a little patch of gray on top," she said. "I believe that's my badge; I earned it." She admits having made some poor choices now and then, "usually in men," but her powerful intuition has given meaningful direction to her and many others.

Intuition is woven into Gini's entire path as a Woman of Destiny. Its messages were a great comfort to her the day she received her own cancer diagnosis, and like always, her gut spoke the truth. Married to an oncologist, Gini was no stranger to the world of cancer statistics, prognoses, and treatment, but sitting in a Manhattan doctor's office as a patient put things in a chilling new perspective. "There were three doctors, one nurse, and a box of tissues sitting in the room when they gave me the bad news," she said. "While they were talking I heard another voice, and I know it was the voice of God. 'You will survive,' the voice said. 'You will do fine, but it's going to be the biggest challenge of your life.'"

The doctors told her she had stage-three breast cancer and about six months to live. The peace of her intuitive message pushed away much of her fear and she decided to trust the voice and the feeling of assuredness that went along with it. "It was real clear; it was going to be tough," she said. "But from that moment, instead of worrying about when I was going to die, I used that time to live." She walked out of the office and met her mom in the waiting room. "I said, 'Okay, Mom, let's go.' She wanted to know what happened and I said, 'I've got cancer, and it's bad, so where do you want to have lunch?' That was a little crazy, but that's how I chose to deal with it. A couple of days later I cried like a baby, but I know what I heard and I told myself that I was going to trust it and move forward."

Twenty-one years later, in 2010, Gini was still moving forward. Directing her literacy program in Suffolk County, New York, she continues to serve her community like a Woman of Destiny, allowing her heart and intuition to put her where she is needed most. To Gini, trusting intuition is equal to having faith. "I heard God," she said of that day in the doctor's office. "I can't give credit anyplace else. If I spent all of my time worrying about when the cancer might come back, I would be wasting good time. I wasn't going to do that. I've lived my whole life by faith and I've not been disappointed yet."

After beating cancer, Gini was faced with handling her mother's long illness, and her intuition once again made all the difference.

Gini took care of her mother in her own home for a number of years before she died. When her mom was still well enough to get out and about, she often took her on drives because her mom loved to ride. But later Gini had a hard time finding things to occupy the time by her mom's bedside. She knew that her mom loved the yellow roses she had been bringing to her every week for about five years, a sunny bouquet sometimes mixed with pink. Gini didn't even need to call in her order—after all that time the florist had them ready for her to pick up every week. But eventually she had a hard time trying to find things to bring comfort to her mom when they spent quiet hours together. Her mother seemed to be slipping away, unable to hold her attention for long. Gini was not getting through to her and had no idea what it would take to engage her mind, heart, and spirit.

Intuition seems to speak loudest when we get close to the edge, and that's where Gini found herself in the fifth year of her mother's illness, when she needed twenty-four-hour care. Gini was getting unraveled over the stress of working full-time and raising her high-school-age son while trying to spend as much time as possible tending to her mom. A nurse's aide came in whenever Gini was not available, and one Saturday afternoon when the aide came to relieve her for an hour or two, Gini went to a bookstore. She wanted to find something to help her relate to her mother, but as she looked through the parenting section she only found books she had already read. That advice had worked for a time, but she needed something else. Nothing spoke to her, and she felt completely helpless. That's when she asked for guidance. "I said, 'Dear Lord, I know you'll give me what I need.'" She started crying her eyes out, thinking how she would spend hundreds of dollars if she could find the right book, but finally decided to leave because she could not find anything.

> *Intuition seems to speak loudest when*
> *we get close to the edge.*

As she started walking toward the door, something on the "$5 and Under" table caught the corner of her eye. She stopped and looked at the cover of a book that contained a beautiful painting of yellow and soft pink roses in a bouquet. Gina picked up the book, a collection of Emily Dickinson poetry, and sensed that the picture was a message. "I thanked God right there in that store," she said. She bought the book, drove home, released the aide, and sat next to her mom. "I said, 'Mom, I figured it out. You like poetry and I like to read poetry.'" From that day on, Gini read poetry to her every day. "Emily Dickinson was a little heavy," she said, "but I found a way to make it work." She bought more poetry books, and the words did exactly what she hoped they would. Her mother listened, she was present and interested and appreciated every minute of it. Gini believes that she was led to that book in order to begin a special practice that would allow her to interact with her mom in her last weeks.

Intuition played an important role again when Gini's mom entered a hospice and the staff told Gini that she would be gone within fifteen hours. Gini suddenly felt compelled to do something she had never done before—tell her mom a lie. "She needed to hear that my father made a mistake and still loved her," Gini said. "She was brutally hurt by their breakup years before, and I knew this was what she needed." She held her mom in her arms and quietly gave her that gift. Her mom smiled like a schoolgirl and "almost purred because she heard something that made her feel so good," Gini said. "I don't believe in lying, but sometimes you know what you need to do." Her mother died peacefully, shortly after hearing the words that lightened her heart.

People have always been drawn to Gini and her porch, where she is fascinated by the conversation and her friends are inspired by her wisdom and insights. Gini says that amazing things happen in that space, which "seems to be a magic carpet." Intuitive messages do seem magical, but it is our destiny to recognize them as normal, everyday occurrences designed to help us.

WE NEVER KNOW HOW HIGH WE ARE (EXCERPT)

We never know how high we are
Till we are asked to rise
And then if we are true to plan
Our statures touch the skies

—*Emily Dickinson*

DEVELOPING YOUR INTUITION

As Women of Destiny, Gini and others in my life understand that the intuitive form of intelligence is a gift to be taken seriously. We are blessed to have minds that can learn, analyze, and create, but our intuition deserves the same respect. As the famous verse from Proverbs states, "The fear of the Lord is the beginning of wisdom," and one of the Hebrew definitions of "fear," which I apply in this case, is "reverence and awe." To revere and be in awe of the Lord is to have wisdom. *To listen to the awe-inspiring messages of the Holy Spirit, or intuition, is to live in wisdom.* This means putting all our rationalizing aside when a voice tells us something that sounds too ridiculous to believe or comes so softly that we can barely hear it beneath our busy thoughts. How many times have you ignored a hunch, only to look back and see that it was correct? A Woman of Destiny always listens to that still, small voice and keeps developing her ability to hear it.

The simplest way to improve your sensitivity toward your intuition is to get into the habit of being quiet for a few minutes every day. Learn to become comfortable with silence. Entering the season of Women of Destiny means getting your mind, body, and spirit in balance, with intuition included as a combination of all three. It is part of the mind because it is a way of knowing, part of the body because we sense it in our gut, and an aspect of spirit because it is divinely inspired.

> *A Woman of Destiny always listens to that*
> *still, small voice and keeps developing*
> *her ability to hear it.*

I am a very social person, but some of my most important places and spaces have become little corners of my home in which I can be alone and listen. I've had to discipline myself to not only focus on the silence but to not be so busy. My natural inclination is to fill every second, which drives my sons crazy. "Mom!" they'll say on a Saturday morning, "can't we just sleep in? Do we have to get up at eight?" And they're right—the quiet, relaxed times are necessary and very important to balancing out the fast-paced nature of our lives. Parenting has taught me to chill out a little bit. After moving to my Manhattan apartment, I got up very early that first Thanksgiving and took a walk in Central Park. It was an unusually mild November morning, and I took my time, stopping to look at a slope of lawn or ripples on a pond and thank God for the day or to just listen so that God could speak. With the park just one block away, I make it a habit of walking in the morning to clear my head before everyone gets up and I have to start my day. I am becoming comfortable with silence, at least for a few minutes at a time.

Attune yourself to the voice of your intuition by stepping out of the noise at least once a day. You can do this at work by sitting back in your chair, closing your eyes, taking a big breath, and relaxing your shoulders on the exhale, and shifting your focus to your hearing. If you are in a more open space where people can see you and you don't feel comfortable closing your eyes, just relax them and focus on a point below your desk, which will naturally close them partway. If you've been listening to the radio or music on your computer, turn it off.

Focus your attention on the sounds around you instead of on your chattering mind.

Just sit and focus on the sounds around you rather than the thoughts that pester you to answer that e-mail or figure out what to make for dinner. Listen to a phone ring in the distance, someone's chair roll across a plastic mat, or a car drive by outside your window. Maybe you will hear your stomach growl or the second hand tick on your watch or the clock. As I write this, I hear coffee bubbling out of a small opening in the decanter on my desk as if it's under pressure, and I wonder how long it's been making this sound without me noticing it. Stopping to listen to the sounds around me helps me get out of thinking mode and into a more receptive state of mind. I believe that if you take the time to do this every day, you will become more comfortable with the idea that your other senses, especially hearing and sensation, are just as powerful as your sight and your constant fixation on your thoughts and the task at hand. You will be more attentive to a gut response, a hard-to-describe "feeling" that you need to do something or a sudden thought/voice that comes out of the blue with a message that won't let you go. Start by honoring the quiet that comes with focusing your mind on the sounds around you rather than your usual racing thoughts.

Another great place to shift your attention is in the car. While keeping your eye on the road and in all your mirrors, of course, you can also focus your attention on the sounds around you instead of on your chattering mind. I love to daydream in the car and relish the chance to be alone, but I also like to take the opportunity to turn off the radio and switch my ears to the mundane sounds that I ignore otherwise. All of a sudden I am aware of the waterlike swish of the cars passing me in the other direction, each one following the same pattern of soft-loud-soft as it approaches, passes, and rushes away. I hear the rhythmic beat of the road as my wheels cross the seams in the pavement. When I scratch my cheek, I actually hear my skin rubbing against my skin. With every new sound, I am reminded that there is so much more to hear and so much that I automatically block out. I tell myself that I am a better listener, that my ears are open to everything, even the mysterious voice of my intuition.

> *Acknowledging intuition is essential,*
> *but responding to it shows that you are*
> *willing to trust and integrate*
> *this tool into your life.*

The next step in becoming more attuned to your intuitive side is to follow the same brief, quiet moments described above with a focus on your sense of touch rather than hearing. Sitting back in your chair at your desk, notice how heavy your arms feel against whatever they are resting upon. Tell yourself to relax your jaw and feel it glide downward. Feel your pulse in your eyes. Does the air flowing into your nose as you inhale feel cool or warm? I am always amazed at how vibrant these sensations are when I take a moment to focus my attention on them. While driving, I stop my inner dialogue for a minute and focus on how my hand feels as it grips the steering wheel. Are my legs comfortable or stiff? When I relax my shoulders, how far down do they move? (I'm tempted to think about why they were so high up and tense in the first place, but then make myself get back to focusing on a sensation.) Does the road feel bumpy, rough, or smooth as it glides beneath me?

Another effective way to develop your intuition is to act on every hunch, gut feeling, or idea that this gift brings to you. Acknowledging intuition is essential, but responding to it shows that you are willing to trust and integrate this tool into your life. Force yourself to stay with the message or feeling rather than let it slip away. You may find, like I have, that your intuitive hunches are not always about you. If someone pops into your mind, try to call her or him—this person may be thinking of you or in need of some kind of help at that moment. If the idea of visiting a store flashes into your mind, go; you may run into someone who needs to speak to you or vice versa. When you follow your hunches you go where you are supposed to go and see who you are supposed to see. It is often a very subtle thing, but that's how intuition works.

You can afford five or ten minutes out of your day to sit quietly and move your attention to your hearing and sensation. This simple practice will help you fine tune your ability to hear the information that is always there, as natural as breathing. By developing this aspect of your intelligence, you will have an indispensable resource to help guide you through your new projects and priorities as a Woman of Destiny.

THE GIFT OF INTUITION

DISCUSSION QUESTIONS

1. Are you more comfortable with a "worldly" or spiritual definition of intuition? Or do you think that the experience is a combination of the two?
2. Why is it relevant that there is scientific proof that we can "see" and respond to emotional events before they occur?
3. Describe an experience or two in which your intuition alerted you to something or gave you a message.
4. Do you feel particularly "in tune" with someone?
5. How do you already use your intuition?

BOOKS ON INTUITION RECOMMENDED

BY MY DESTINY CIRCLE:

_____

_____

_____

_____

_____

THE GIFT OF INTUITION
√ CHECKLIST

___ Consider the idea that intuition is a natural, God-given gift and one aspect of my intelligence. Acknowledge that intuition is real, worthy of my attention, and a valuable resource for guidance.

___ Take the time to be quiet for a few minutes every day. Become comfortable with silence.

___ Intuition exercise #1: Spend five minutes every other day simply listening to the sounds around me, being aware of them instead of the usual chatter of my mind.

___ Intuition exercise #2: Spend five minutes on alternate days sitting quietly and being aware of touch sensations—body tension, air temperature, vibrations, or movement in the car—instead of the usual chatter of my mind.

___ Intuition exercise #3: Acknowledge and act on hunches and messages that pop into my mind. Trust the information and follow through.

MY PILLAR II CONTRACT WITH DESTINY

I am a spiritual being with an ever-deepening relationship to God. My life is in balance with an active inner *and* outer life because I make time for prayer and reflection. As a Woman of Destiny, the richness of my spirituality brings insight, compassion, and energy to everything I do.

PILLAR III:
ACTION

Real integrity is doing the right thing, knowing that nobody's
going to know whether you did it or not.

—OPRAH WINFREY

A DESTINY WOMAN'S PRAYER FOR ACTION

This is the day you have made, O God. Not only will I REJOICE in
you, but also I ask that I may I go FORWARD in you. Your movement
has always been an action that takes us from where we have BEEN to
where you would have us BE. But I also must do my part. I ask you for
the strength to make the moves that you have given to me—to know that
there is NOTHING that you and I cannot do together. I believe and
declare the MOMENT is NOW. I was made for this moment. Help me
walk into my DESTINED path, trusting you every step of the way. You
have held my hand and had my back. Today I take the steps to fly, as
you are the wind beneath my wings. I'm Ready. I'm Strong. I'm Yours.
Thank you, Lord. Amen.

Chapter Six

THE WISDOM OF INTEGRITY

Deborah was a leader in the time before Israel had its first kings, so her behavior as a judge and counselor set the ethical standard for her people. She never allowed herself to be corrupted but followed the hallowed traditions of honesty and fairness that had been handed down to judges from the time of Moses.

A Woman of Destiny is a model of integrity in her community because of the way she conducts herself with others—showing respect to everyone that comes before her and promoting cooperation. Her integrity also comes through in the way she manages her own affairs, bringing as much respect and honesty to the details of her private affairs as she does to her public life.

Like Deborah, women in transition show their honorable character by listening respectfully to both sides of an issue and making sound judgments. They shine as beacons of integrity and honesty in the world by pursuing their goals with high personal standards.

Under Deborah's leadership, the Israelites were united in action for the first time, and it worked. In unity they found strength. Women of Destiny make a powerful impact in groups of all kinds, from families to communities, by looking for connections rather than differences and pointing out people's unique gifts. Putting high ethical standards into action inspires, motivates, and instructs, and everyone who comes into contact with a Woman of Destiny is transformed.

SHE'S GOT CHARACTER: THE GRACEFULNESS OF RESPECT

Only people of the strongest character could be judges, the "rulers over thousands" in Deborah's time (Exodus 18:21). Among the character traits that elevated Deborah to the status of judge were the confidence and maturity that allowed her to respect others' roles, opinions, and ideas. Judges were known as people of truth who hated "covetousness," or a yearning to have what others have. The opposite of yearning is feeling secure in oneself. A woman of Deborah's character did not envy, resent, or feel jealous or intimidated; instead, she approached every person with gracious peacefulness and respect that comes with utter confidence in oneself.

> *Power is what you do and character is what you are.*
>
> ∽∾
>
> —*Richard Reeves, presidential historian and journalist*

The virtues that Deborah holds up for us to follow are also described in the Gospel of James, which lists the qualities of "the wisdom from above," an intelligence melded with spirituality. This balanced wisdom is "pure, then peaceable, gentle, willing to yield, full of mercy and good fruits, without a trace of partiality or hypocrisy." Someone who has not developed those qualities but feels "yearnings" for things outside herself is in conflict with the world. "Those conflicts and disputes among you, where do they come from? Do they not come from your cravings that are at war within you? . . . You covet something and cannot obtain it; so you engage in disputes and conflicts" (James 3:17; 4:1–2).

Those verses help us understand how Deborah calls us to be peaceful and secure rather than envious and conflicted. As Women of Destiny, we respect others and ourselves out of the confidence and security that comes with maturity. Treating others with respect reflects character.

One of the people who taught me about this important aspect of character was my late mother, Dorothy Johnson, who was a woman of great respect throughout her life. As I was cleaning out her apartment I found many cards from people who thanked her because of what she had done for them. She saw the best in people, regardless of their circumstances, and helped as many as she could reach their potential. Some of the cards were from people she had put through nursing or law school. She taught me at her knee how to show respect. She worked with winos and those on welfare. "You speak to everyone," she would tell me, "because they're all human beings."

Another person who taught me about respect is Bishop Desmond Tutu, whom I have met several times. When I was in South Africa, after he had been made the Anglican Archbishop, there had been an incident with fighting in the streets. I watched the news story on TV, which showed Bishop Tutu walking into the midst of the fight. Troops and tribes who hated each other stopped in their tracks. His presence commanded the respect that made them say, "We have to stop what we're doing." That incident will always stay with me.

If you could only love enough, you could be the most powerful person in the world.

—*The Reverend Emmet Fox*

I learned more about the power and graciousness of respect when I worked on then–Senator Hillary Clinton's presidential

BECOMING A WOMAN OF DESTINY

campaign in 2008. The organizations that succeeded in booking her as a speaker reacted like it was the coup of all time. When she walked into a room at a 1,500-person event in a grand ballroom, people would break their necks to get close. She earned a lot of respect as a First Lady who had the chutzpah to take on health care reform, which made her a trailblazer on very rough terrain, and then to run for and win the U.S. Senate seat from New York. It was amazing to watch her take on so much responsibility and command so much respect during her presidential race. She had a strong circle of successful women around her, but it was clear who was the powerful and influential woman. Nobody voted; it was deferred to her. It was wonderful.

Senator Clinton earned the respect of millions, but she was just as respectful of others. She trusted and respected me enough to name me a surrogate for her campaign, someone who would be her principal spokesperson at events. When she needed to be in two places at once, I would be one of the surrogates she entrusted to speak for her in that state. I felt like I was carrying china—I didn't want to make any wrong moves because I didn't want to let her down.

One of her last stops on the campaign was in North Carolina, a deciding state near the end when they were figuring out whether or not she would continue in the primaries. I got a call from Bill Clinton's office asking if I could join them in the motorcade going to North Carolina. We drove to the state and then flew to four cities. My job that day was not only to speak on Senator Clinton's behalf but also to introduce President Clinton and a governor who was with us. When we landed and set up in a field near

Newbern, I realized that I was standing where my mother's hands had picked cotton and tobacco. And there I was, introducing a former president of the United States. It was a moment of utmost respect for my mother that said, "We don't have to be in the fields in the same way anymore; we step in them with presidents instead of kneel in them."

Black people talk a lot about their ancestors, and at that moment my whole ancestry welled up in me. We had a saying, "Remember who you are." You do your best in life to pull up yourself, and by doing that you pull up all the people who paved the way for you to have all your opportunities. The Clinton family showed respect for me by inviting me to travel and speak for them at that level, and I knew that that was a moment for my entire ancestry.

Another icon of respect whose path I was honored to cross was Coretta Scott King. Her children showed their respect for the friendship Mrs. King and I had shared by asking me to officiate at her funeral. The respect she commanded, even in death, was amazing. When we rode through her community, the people were lined up for miles to pay their respects as her car passed by. It was only the third time in the history of Georgia that someone was laid in state in the capitol in Atlanta.

I recalled how twelve thousand people at the Hampton Ministers' Conference had shown their respect when she walked out on stage with me—a hush fell over the massive room. She helped draw people from all over the world to that conference. Her presence was her present.

My mother, Hillary Clinton, and Mrs. King all lived out the virtue of respectfulness, including respectful listening. Politicians like Secretary of State Clinton are masters of analyzing all sides of an issue in order to create law and policy, just as Deborah was. My mother showed me the patience, compassion, and respect of Deborah when she listened to a transient man at her door with the same courtesy she showed our pastor when he sat at her dinner table. By seeing respect in action in many forms through the lives of these women, I learned that it is truly possible to live like Deborah and become a Woman of Destiny.

A consistently respectful attitude can take as much discipline to develop as a spiritual practice.

In day-to-day life, treating everyone we meet with respect takes work—it does not always come naturally. A consistently respectful attitude can take as much discipline to develop as a spiritual practice. Living in New York City makes it a real challenge at times, especially when rushing through errands like grocery shopping. Sometimes the clerks aren't the sunniest people in the world, and when I'm tempted to think badly of a clerk's shortness with me I try to remember what my mother taught me. Then I say to myself, "Of course this young woman is feeling cranky; she probably earns very little for working long hours and putting up with demanding New Yorkers hour after hour." When I take the time to fix my attitude like that, I open my heart and give her a smile and a "thank you" and really mean it. People can feel it when you mean it, and they can see it in your eyes. Just saying a genuine thank you can be a gesture of respect that helps light up someone's day.

> *Just saying a genuine thank you can be a*
> *gesture of respect that helps light up*
> *someone's day.*

Honoring people with respect in the little things adds up week after week and year after year to stronger character. Having character, being a person of respect and integrity who people can always count on, makes us fit for more responsibilities and opportunities. As Les Brown wrote in *Live Your Dreams*, "You must be willing to do the things today others won't do in order to have the things tomorrow others won't have." He was writing about more material goals, but it applies to "doing things" to build your character as well. If you're willing to improve your attitude in the checkout line; listen carefully and consider both sides of an issue at work, even when you are much more personally invested in one; or simply take five minutes to put down your newspaper and listen to an elderly man on the bus who needs someone to talk to, you may "have" something tomorrow like the respect of more people than you had before.

BE A UNIFIER

Deborah's call to battle, which brought ten thousand men from the scattered tribes of Israel together, was the strategy that brought forty years of peace to her people. Only in unity could they muster up a force that Sisera would take seriously enough to engage on the plain below Mount Tabor.

I grew up in an Italian and Jewish neighborhood in the northeast Bronx where black families were slowly moving in. It was a very integrated neighborhood and Pastor William Farrell of Eastchester Presbyterian Church had a way of bringing the different ethnicities together. There were historical tensions to deal with because people had heard that black people from Harlem were this and that and the Caribbean people spoke with a dialect that was too hard to understand. The church was the unifying place where we came together and found common ground. We were told that Jesus loves all of us, and after church black, Italian, and Caribbean children would walk home together.

Our neighbors right next door in the row houses were the Tanzellas. My mother and Mrs. Tanzella would pass food across the stoop to each other—Mrs. T would send over some lasagna and Mom would give her some collard greens. They made an extra dish for each other's family and brought it out, with mitts on, right from the oven. Then conversation would begin, "How's your daughter, your son?"

> *As we express our gratitude, we must never forget that the highest appreciation is not to utter words, but to live by them.*
>
> —*John F. Kennedy*

Living in that neighborhood was the beginning of a new season for me, a boundaryless kind of life that made me want to learn about other cultures. Mrs. T's lasagna was serious. It was like a peace offering, an act that said, "Let me pass a piece of something that's special to me and give it to you. Not leftovers, but fresh food I'm making for my family. I'm trying to find a way to connect with you." The children could then say, "We don't know much about each other, but our mothers know how to cook. Let's start there." As simple as it sounds, in this world everybody has to agree to start somewhere.

Church taught me about making connections with groups in the neighborhood and with other cultural perspectives within the black community. Mom was Presbyterian and Dad was Baptist, so every Sunday my brother and I went to Sunday school at East-chester Presbyterian and then took the bus down to Harlem to join our parents' churches, Rendall Memorial Presbyterian and Union Baptist (where I would later enter the ministry). People loved up on us at each church and we grew up being part of three extended church families. My childhood was filled with men and women who modeled the importance of finding connections instead of being put off by differences.

Making connections and building integrated communities was going on in other parts of the country, and a story about Reverend John Rice in Denver in the 1970s shows how one person can help an entire group start to think outside the box. As Antonia Felix writes in her biography *Condi: The Condoleezza Rice Story*, Reverend Rice, father of future Secretary of State Condoleezza Rice, taught at the University of Denver and was an associate pastor at a predominantly white Presbyterian church in the city. The church was very proactive in helping integrate the neighborhood and wanted to attract more blacks to its congregation. In a meeting about that effort, Reverend Rice asked them if they all agreed about integration. The parishioners said yes. He then asked where the nearest black Presbyterian church was, and they said it was a couple of miles away. "Why don't some of you join it?" Rice asked. The room went silent as the members realized how one-sided their idea of integration had been.

I recently moderated a conference attended by women from many different fields, including a vice president of Universal Studios, a retired judge, a state senator, and someone who worked with Habitat for Humanity. To start the discussion, I asked them four questions:

1. What got you to this moment?
2. How do you keep yourself together (self-preservation)?
3. With whom do you surround yourself?
4. What legacy do you hope to leave?

They each got ten minutes to respond, and it was powerfully moving. The common denominator for every single woman was family, the role that the strength of family played in their lives. In sharing our stories we found common ground as leading women. Finding strong, new connections based on common ground was important at that point in my life because with the recent death of my brother I had lost my entire immediate family. That was a major paradigm shift for me, and forming new bonds was critical.

Deborah's role as a unifier is a message about the gifts that unfold when we look for common ground. As Women of Destiny, we are challenged to emphasize connection and cooperation. This attitude applies to relating to family, work, organizations, and the support systems that we create for ourselves.

HONORING OUR OBLIGATIONS

The integrity, respectfulness, and talent for unifying that made Deborah a revered judge and leader were not her only noble qualities. Honesty and transparency were also important for someone in a position where bribes or other backdoor deals could corrupt the system. As the sole leader, teacher, spiritual guide, and judge of her people, Deborah had to live an exemplary life that kept to the highest ethical standards.

Deborah inspires us to take stock of how honestly we approach our relationships, both personal and professional. And just as important, her example asks us to look at the honesty we bring to our personal finances and other obligations. In our public lives we have constant reminders about the costs of dishonesty or shoddy behavior—laws, being judged by others who catch us in a dishonest act, shame. This gives us even more motivation to always take the right path. But when it comes to our record keeping and bills at home, we may be tempted to be less organized or efficient. If no one is looking, why keep perfect track of receipts? Why spend an hour or two researching the best price for a new appliance when it's easier to just go to the nearest store and buy it? Why write up a household budget when your checking account balance is easy to find online and you think you can keep track of your spending in your head?

I believe that Women of Destiny are called to bring the same careful attention and transparency to their personal finances and household records that they give to their professional obligations. By keeping this part of our lives in order, there are no loose ends to drain us of our energy or nag us in the middle of the night. With bills and the budget, just like everything else, if you are not in control of it, it is in control of you. It is easy to let things get disorganized when you are the only one paying attention to them, but that attitude takes away from your overall integrity. Bringing careful attention and integrity to every obligation in your life is the path that Deborah invites you to follow.

> *There is no pillow so soft as a clear conscience.*
>
> —*French proverb*

A respectful attitude toward your personal obligations goes hand-in-hand with honoring your time. Settled in her designated space beneath her palm tree, Deborah calls people to her and reminds us that we don't need to rush around and be reckless with our time.

Life is more than bills, but you have to take the time to write them, negotiate then, take a bath, and have a meal without rushing. You have to take some time to think and pray if you're always moving 365 days a year at the same pace, otherwise your body will respond in illness or fatigue or you will not get things done to the best of your ability.

When I look at Deborah, our sister, she rules under the palm tree of Deborah between two holy cities. She didn't run herself ragged; she allowed others to come to her. We've done enough running to others, for others; now it's time to sit and be alone. This goes for being out and about by yourself, enjoying your own company from time to time. Gwendolyn Grant, who used to write a column for *Ebony* magazine, would say, "I'm going out *with* myself, not *by* myself." Find a restaurant where you are not likely to run into people you know so that you can spend an enjoyable time out with yourself (and not be put in the awkward situation of having to say no if someone invites you to their table).

Create privacy and relaxation at home by turning off your cell phone and letting everyone in your life know when your "office hours" are over. These self-preservation boundaries help you retain the integrity and 100 percent energy you want to bring to the activities that you have so carefully selected for the new season of your life. You will avoid burnout, which I have experienced and would not wish on anyone. I do not wish to repeat that lesson because maturity is about integrating an experience and helping others avoid some of the problems you overcame.

Deborah was the ultimate multitasker—wife, judge, leader, prophet, and spiritual guide. When we throw military strategist into the mix, she might seem too far beyond us, but I doubt that her schedule was any fuller than those of today's working wives, mothers, and professional women. The commitments and responsibilities we take on can quickly get out of control and leave us without enough time, energy, or focus to do any one them well. A Woman of Destiny must treat her schedule with respect and learn to say no. One of my mottos is "No is a complete sentence." Once you have made up your mind about the work and obligations of your new season, stick to the schedule that you have so thoughtfully set up. It is not rude or inappropriate to tell someone that you do not want to get involved in his project. Treating ourselves with respect includes honoring the new goals and activities we have carefully chosen for this season.

*One of my favorite mottos is
"No is a complete sentence."*

THE WISDOM OF INTEGRITY

DISCUSSION QUESTIONS

1. When is the last time you felt envious of someone? What did they possess that you wanted?
2. American culture does not have any formal gestures or customs for expressing respect. How do you show respect to someone, such as an elderly relative?
3. Whom do you admire for his or her integrity, and how is it expressed?
4. Has anyone returned something to you that you lost, or vice versa? Recall how you felt in either case.
5. When did you most recently do "the right thing" even though no one else knew about it?
6. What is your comfort level for saying no?
7. Do you have a household budget on paper? How organized are your bills and important papers?

BOOKS ON INTEGRITY RECOMMENDED BY MY DESTINY CIRCLE:

_____

_____

_____

_____

_____

THE WISDOM OF INTEGRITY

√ **CHECKLIST**

___ Pay attention to feelings of envy or jealousy and reflect on why I want what I do not have.

___ Show respect for everyone I meet, even those who do not treat me respectfully.

___ Write up a household budget and record my expenses.

___ Organize my bills and papers.

___ Bring together a few friends and give each a few minutes to answer four questions, then discuss our common ground.

1. What got you to this moment?
2. How do you keep yourself together (self-care/preservation)?
3. With whom do you surround yourself?
4. What legacy do you hope to leave?

Chapter Seven

GIVING BACK TO BUILD
A NEW WORLD

I n 2007, the Tate Modern in London opened an exhibit of works by Paris-born American painter and sculptor Louise Bourgeois, one of our era's most important artists. The retrospective included her latest masterworks that put raw human emotion into abstract sculptural forms, the follow-ups to her most ambitious work, a thirty-foot-high giant spider she had sculpted a few years earlier *at age eighty-eight*. Still going strong during the new Tate exhibition at age ninety-five, Bourgeois is just one of many women artists who are doing their best work in their sixties and beyond.

Novelist E. Annie Proulx (pronounced "Pru") published her second novel, *The Shipping News,* at the age of fifty-eight, and the book won the Pulitzer Prize for fiction and the National Book Award the next year. One of her short stories, "Brokeback Mountain," became an Academy Award–winning movie in 2005 when Proulx was seventy.

Four months before her fiftieth birthday, Katie Couric took over as anchor and managing editor of the *CBS Evening News,* making her the first woman solo news anchor of a network evening news show.

Nancy Pelosi had been active in Democratic politics while raising her five children in New York and San Francisco, but she did not launch her career in earnest and run for political office until her youngest was a senior in high school. In 1987, at age forty-seven, she was elected to represent California's Eighth District in the U.S. House of Representatives and has been reelected ever since. She was sixty-two when her party elected her the House Minority Leader, which put her in the history books as the first woman to hold that powerful position.

In *Women Who Mean Business: Success Stories of Women over Forty*, A. Mikaelian tells the stories of seventy-five women in their forties and fifties who hold high-profile positions. Despite their very different stories, they meet on common ground over one issue: "Regardless of their profession, education, or background," Mikaelian wrote, "all of these professionals share a commitment to improving their world through community service."

Businesswomen, artists, writers, and mature women in all kinds of other fields do their best work after fifty. Rather than slowing down, they enter the second half of life with irreplaceable skills, experience, and insights that can now go into their work.

LISTENING TO WOMEN'S VOICES:
A NEW ERA FOR WOMEN OF DESTINY

Holding up the stories of women like Bourgeois, Proulx, Couric, Pelosi, and all the women who been "firsts" in their fields reminds us that successful, impactful women seem to be the exception. They are trailblazers in a world where most of the prominent art and leadership is done by men. But I believe that the great strides that women have made over the past two hundred years have led to a very special moment for women, the start of a new era in which women sharing the same stages as men—in equal numbers—is the norm. In this new era, women's input is equally important and honored. This is the age of Women of Destiny, in which mature women are honored and recognized as crucial resources whose experience, energy, compassion, skills, and insights bring solutions where none could be found before and make the world a better place. Society becomes accustomed to hearing women's voices as frequently as those of men. This new era is a reflection of the ancient matriarchal cultures in which no gender was in charge but both had an equal say. It is truly democratic, benefiting from male perspectives and energies as well as the unique experiences and wisdom that women bring.

This is the era that Women of Destiny have been called to bring forth. By walking confidently into your new season, you offer gifts to your community in two ways: bringing the value of your work itself and bringing a wise and strong woman's voice into the mix.

> *This is the age of Women of Destiny, in which mature women are honored and recognized as crucial resources whose experience, energy, compassion, skills, and insights bring solutions where none could be found before and make the world a better place.*

The long study of matriarchal cultures is controversial because there has been some misunderstanding about what a matriarchy was—and continues to be in some parts of the world. Researchers tell us that a matriarchy is not a society in which women rule over men and men become second-class citizens. Instead, matriarchies are all about equality. Decisions in family clans and between larger groups are made by consensus in these societies. One gender or family or political group does not have power over another.

> *The role of women . . . does point to the radical social reality constituted by the Jesus movement in first-century Palestine. . . . It was a "discipleship of equals" embodying . . . Jesus' vision.*
>
> —*Marcus J. Borg,* Meeting Jesus Again for the First Time

Women do, however, have the upper hand when it comes to dividing up the fields and food that nourish their clans. Why do these cultures give that responsibility to women? That's one of the ongoing topics of debate. But in every other sense of the word, matriarchies are true democracies. In our country, on the other hand, women only made up 20 percent of the U.S. Congress in early 2010, far less than the 50 percent that would be truly democratic. The facts are the facts; women do not have as much of a voice in making the rules that create our society.

By working on each stage of the path to becoming a Woman of Destiny, you are bringing this idea of equal voices—and the value of maturity—back to life in the world. Aging is still something people would rather not talk about because we are constantly told by ads and TV shows and movies that youth is the most beautiful reflection of what it means to be human. But I believe that we are ready to embrace the beauty of mature wisdom, energy, creativity, and priorities. Our culture may have ignored mature women for most of its history, but the time is ripe for changing that. That is the exciting cultural role of Women of Destiny.

> *In everyone's life, at some time, our inner fire goes out. It is then burst into flame by an encounter with another human being.*
> *We should all be thankful for those people who rekindle the inner spirit.*
>
> —*Albert Schweitzer*

During the action phase of your journey, your life is dedicated to pouring your newfound strengths and passions into the world. This new life is only possible because of the intense work you did to assess where you were and where you wanted to go through the Season II exercise and the reflective processes that went with it. That assessment period is absolutely necessary, and brings order to a time of life that can be very chaotic. Many women coming in to the second half of life feel that they are too young to retire because they still have big obligations, like children in college, but at the same time they cannot envision themselves in the same place at age sixty-two. Staying with the status quo is not fair to women who have much more to give, nor is it fair to their families or communities that could benefit so much more from the work and energy that a Woman of Destiny offers.

Following through with your strategies for taking on your new roles, you are now ready to do the work that your entire life has prepared you for.

For some this is creating art or writing books, for others becoming politically active or an expert spokesperson on an important issue. Some will give speeches and presentations about their journeys in order to inspire others to take up new goals in the second half of life. Others will focus on their friends and families, providing emotional support for someone in pain or convincing a grandchild to stay in school. Those who are entering a new season of an established career will infuse their work with new confidence, energy, creativity, and wisdom that will have a fresh new impact on the job and everyone involved.

GIVING BACK

Just before my mother passed, she sent me a card that read, "To the woman who knows where she is going." It was as though she believed that all she had deposited into me had taken root, that the Woman of Destiny she was had been properly transferred or conferred upon me. Passing wisdom along is connected to another life lesson I gained from my mother. The larger message is about using our gifts to enrich and give back to the world.

My mother and grandmother were the first to teach me the biblical call to give back: "Unto whomsoever much is given, of him shall be much required" (Luke 12:48, KJV). That sense of responsibility seeped in and stayed with me, especially when I saw my parents put it into action. My mother, who was a school-teacher in Harlem, brought children home every weekend so that they could eat with us, sleep with us, and be part of our family. We were not rich, but we had a better quality of life than most of her students knew and she wanted to expose them to another way of life. My parents bought shoes for children, found work for people, and gave whatever they could to whoever needed it. If their combined income was $100 more than anyone else on the block, they made sure that every dollar of that $100 was shared.

> *The time is always right to do what is right.*
>
> —*Martin Luther King, Jr.*

My family also taught me early on that my life had a special purpose. Mom and Grandmother backed up their belief that my brother and I could do anything we put our minds to with the words of Paul: "All things work together for good to them that love God, to them who are the called according to his purpose" (Romans 8:28, KJV). I never took my opportunities for granted but felt that I was being prepared for a calling. And there was no doubt that whatever my calling turned out to be it would include avenues for giving back and serving others.

> *One thing that never ceases to amaze me, along with the growth of vegetation from earth and hair from the head, is the growth of understanding.*
>
> —*Alice Walker*

After decades in the ministry and new, related ventures in the works, I was thrilled with the idea that one part of my calling involved showing other women how to be Women of Destiny.

This book is part of my journey as a Woman of Destiny, a call for others to celebrate midlife and other life transitions as stimulating turning points that will lead them to their greatest fulfillment. In turn, more women will appreciate their well-earned experience, honor their passions, and move forward to give their unique gifts to the world.

A Destiny Fulfilled . . . and More to Come

When I sat down and took stock of my future during that life-changing moment we call turning fifty, I knew that I wanted to stay in the ministry but not in the same way. I opened myself up to new ideas by paying attention to the desires that I had put on hold, such as being more of a performer (I wanted to go into acting when I went to college as a communications major) and a producer (I loved bringing talented people together). Assessing those skills and passions, I imagined what preaching would look like if it fused them into one experience. I took all my talents that were begging to be used and thought out of the box to create something new. The result was an interdenominational, cross-cultural, dramatic production known as Harlem Hallelujah.

This one-hour service, which I booked at the famous Apollo Theater on 125th Street in Harlem, was modeled on my lunchtime Wall Street programs and expanded to include a larger variety of inspirational "acts" including dance, speakers, choirs, a message, interviews with inspiring people from diverse fields, and more.

Some of the obstacles I faced while getting this production off the ground came from surprising places. The pastor of a large New York church criticized the concept in his pulpit the week before my first service. Without mentioning my name, he talked about services going up at the Apollo Theater, which wasn't right because "worship should be at worship's place." That was said in front of about a thousand people, many of whom were my friends and knew exactly who he was talking about. But I understood that some people hold on to tradition closely and let their insecurities speak first. I did not take his remarks seriously when I heard about them but trusted my own vision. I had worked diligently and creatively to find my new place and prayed, "God, use me for this season wherever you see fit." Without a doubt, God's answer was Harlem Hallelujah.

> *Every great dream begins with a dreamer. Always remember, you have within you the strength, the patience, and the passion to reach for the stars to change the world.*
>
> —*Harriet Tubman*

Finding sponsors was another challenge in launching the project. Even though the Apollo is a landmark venue and world-famous icon, the word "worship" made it difficult to get financial backing from corporations and some businesses. I sensed that they feared there would be fallout for aligning the company or organization with religion, which I could understand. Those challenges motivated me to look in new directions and step out of my comfort zone to ask everyone I could think of to pitch in and sponsor part of the production. That tenaciousness paid off and I pulled together the financing to launch the series.

We advertised and designed Harlem Hallelujah as a response to the tough times, an "Inspiration for the Nation" that would nourish and help attendees get through the next stress-filled week. That message hit the right chord, because we filled up that theater week after week. People of all races and faiths, from every borough and even other states and countries flocked to subsequent services as word spread about the event. People from black and white churches in New York came to see what we were up to, and they kept coming back because they were inspired. Some people came because they had always wanted to see the Apollo. Others came because Harlem's 125th Street was in their New York City tourist guidebook. People came for many reasons, like I knew they would.

I branched out to Washington, D.C., in the summer of 2009 with Wonderful Washington Worship, a thirty-minute midday service in the heart of the nation's capital like the one I had created in lower Manhattan. Every Tuesday for seven weeks we packed people into a church on Massachusetts and Ninth Streets for a fast-paced, uplifting service that would give them, I prayed, a little more hope than they woke up with that morning.

I created Harlem Hallelujah because I believed that the

Apollo Theater could draw people together through faith, and our success gave me the courage to dream even bigger and bring the service to a wider global audience through TV and tours. My women's conference has become an international event, and I hope to do the same with the Apollo services.

> *The most important thing to remember is this:*
> *To be ready at any moment to give up what you*
> *are for what you might become.*
>
> —*W. E. B. Du Bois*

Each project I have launched has become the springboard for something else that I had not envisioned when I started listening to my neglected dreams and began the journey of becoming a Woman of Destiny. When you begin delivering your new gifts and interacting with the world as a Woman of Destiny, you will find that the options are endless because there are so many ways to bring together the skills, dreams, interests, and experiences you have gathered and earned in the first five decades of your life. In the action stage, you will continue to assess where you are and where you want to go next. You will reinvent yourself again and again while the world blossoms under your feet.

GIVING BACK TO BUILD A NEW WORLD
DISCUSSION QUESTIONS

1. What are you able to contribute as you continue to move through your twenties, thirties, forties, fifties, and beyond?

2. Why do you think fewer women than men run for public office?

3. Did your parents have a sense of responsibility toward the community, or did they limit their resources to the family? How has that affected your approach to the Woman of Destiny's call to give back?

4. Describe one of your talents/skills and the responsibility you feel toward it.

5. Describe the most striking transformations you have made in your life thus far; how have you reinvented yourself? What new direction did each change bring about?

BOOKS ON GIVING BACK RECOMMENDED
BY MY DESTINY CIRCLE:

_____

_____

_____

_____

_____

GIVING BACK TO BUILD A NEW WORLD
√ **CHECKLIST**

___ Remind myself every day that:

MY BEST WORK IS STILL AHEAD OF ME

and

MATURE INSIGHT AND EXPERIENCE IS OF GREAT VALUE TO SOCIETY.

___ Make a list of people and organizations that have played an important role in my life and reflect on what I can give in return: my expertise, contribution of time or money, or an endorsement?

___ List places in which I can share my expertise through a talk or presentation, such as local schools and organizations.

___ When I come across an obstacle while putting my new role into action, respond with patience, clarity, perseverance, respectfulness, and integrity. I will listen to my intuition and honor the goals and strategies I have carefully designed.

MY PILLAR III CONTRACT WITH DESTINY

My respect for others is a living reflection of the respect I have for myself. I honor every person I meet and every task put before me with integrity because it is a privilege to work, interact, love, and simply be alive. The time has come for me and other Women of Destiny to radiate our wisdom and mindfulness into the world as only we can do.

PILLAR IV: COMMUNITY

Come out of the circle of time, and into the circle of love.

—RUMI, thirteenth-century Persian poet

A DESTINY WOMAN'S PRAYER FOR COMMUNITY

O God, how grateful I am that you have made me a woman that other women can feel close to. Thank you for your mentoring spirit of favor, love, and grace that you have shadowed and showered upon me. As the anointing that was upon Peter's life in the book of Acts and Deborah's in the book of Judges, may your spirit of holiness, hospitality, wonder, and wisdom fall upon me. When others are around me, may they feel and see you. As I speak, may the words upon my lips reflect your love. May the meditations of my heart be inviting so that others may want to come closer to you. Help me to bring the women together. Help me to show your love. Amen.

Chapter Eight

CREATING COMMUNITY

The journey that women travel in order to move productively into each new season of life is not a solitary path. At the same time that our actions lead us into new areas of work and expression, we come together with each other to bring our soul work into community. The final step in mapping out your new season is designing a new way to nurture and be nurtured in your Destiny Circle.

Coming together with a group of kindred spirits is essential, nourishing, invigorating, soulful, and enlightening. Paul tells us that the older women in the community are "teachers of good things" (Titus 2:3, KJV), and Women of Destiny are most fulfilled when they can share each other's wisdom. The Destiny Circle is a private group that gathers for mentoring, collaborating, sustaining, validating, and encouraging each member. This is not therapy or a place to vent complaints, but a carefully established, safe forum for being authentic, enthusiastic, and generous about your nature. Only here can you benefit from others who share a commitment to building new goals in the second half of life and find a wealth of insight and experience free from the limitations of other organizations. The agenda is flexible and unique to each group, honoring the intellectual, spiritual, and social aspects of a life lived as a Woman of Destiny.

CIRCLES THAT MATTER

The Destiny Circle is patterned after a women's group I started about fifteen years ago after the death of a friend's mother. I went out to lunch with another friend and said, "Sage's mother just died, she needs someone. Let's invite some people to breakfast." We called up about a dozen women aged about thirty-five to seventy-five from various professions and scheduled a get-together for an early Friday morning. In preparation, I told them when I called that we were just going to tell our stories. Each person would introduce herself and tell us about one thing she wants to celebrate and one thing she wants prayers for. Each person would get her chance to share those three things.

> *Coming together with a group of kindred spirits is essential, nourishing, invigorating, soulful, and enlightening.*

Everyone had been waiting for this moment. There had been no place to celebrate our accomplishments as women or confide about our needs. We started meeting on a regular basis and allowed each member to invite someone who would benefit from the circle. To make sure that the a new person would be a good fit, someone who could keep the confidentiality of the group, I and the other founding member met with her first. We grew to a group of about thirty, but there were always about a dozen who made each meeting.

We named the group the Isis Circle after the Egyptian queen who called on her sister to help her gather up all the pieces of her husband who had been killed. The Nile was the collection of all her tears. The Isis Circle is still going today, and when we meet we pick up the broken parts of our lives. It remained a safe space for sharing important issues and experiences that could not be aired anywhere else. One woman in that first group, for example, was a woman who needed anonymity about some of her deepest concerns.

We now have a retreat in the summer at one member's beach house on Long Island, and we can bring other women. It's almost out of control because so many women want to be part of Isis. We still have not decided if we want to make the circle bigger or allow more younger women under thirty. Some of the older women are concerned about that; they don't think they would be comfortable sharing in front of a daughter's best friend.

The soul-nourishing, heart-opening experiences of the Isis Circle had such a powerful effect on us that I began to use groups in my ministry. I believed that creating circles for the women who gravitated toward certain types of work in the church would facilitate the flow, so I came up with three circles that centered on cooking, audio-visual, and altar work. Each group was assigned to name itself after an African-American hero or biblical woman, research her story, and share the information with everyone. When the women chose their circle, it didn't matter if they didn't know the people sitting next to them at first; they had a similar interest. The groups added a new dynamic to the church and made everyone's experience richer. Women who joined the church quickly found a sense of community by fitting into one of the circles.

I utilized the circle experience again at one of my annual women's conferences as a way to choose where we would hold the next year's meeting. We broke up into three circles that represented three locations. Each group's job was to convince the rest of us why we should choose its locale. They had an hour. This was the first time they had worked together at the conference because everything else had been individual. They came back with posters, cheers, songs, and a feeling of genuine sisterhood. Many said that no one had ever celebrated them before. Women with common issues found out about each other, particularly the cancer survivors. Since then, one survivor has created a ministry to help women who are going through radiation and chemo. When she was going through treatment she liked to take baths with lavender soap, so now she sends baskets of them to cancer patients for free. That beautiful practice grew out of the circle.

> *The love of our neighbor in all its fullness simply means being able to say, "What are you going through?"*
>
> —*Simone Weil*

Another healing circle that rose up on its own came about while I was working on a book of women's devotionals. I went through all my address books and sent out invitations to a hundred women, asking them for personal input about life experiences I was covering in the book. One who replied was my fifth-grade teacher, who wrote a devotional about losing a child. I had heard that her college child had been killed while driving home from camp. She had never talked about it, and in writing this story she was able to share it for the first time. It was healing for her. People who read the book called her and said the same thing had happened to them and they couldn't talk about it. Longing for community and safe space, they started a circle of women who needed to share their grief by connecting through letters.

Healing, encouraging, inspiring, and loving, your own Destiny Circle will become one of the most important spaces you create as you approach any period of transition with the grace, intelligence, and action of a Woman of Destiny.

CREATING COMMUNITY
DISCUSSION QUESTIONS

1. Do you have a friend with whom you connect on a soulful level? How did you find each other?
2. What issue or insight would you share if you were going to a Destiny Circle meeting today?
3. Describe one or two challenges you are facing as you enter your new season that you suspect other women may be experiencing as well.
4. Describe other groups in which you have participated, such as a book club, dinner group, etc. Did it allow you to reach the level of connection with others that you had hoped for?

BOOKS ON FRIENDSHIP AND CONNECTED RECOMMENDED
BY MY DESTINY CIRCLE:

_____

_____

_____

_____

_____

Chapter Nine

FORMING YOUR DESTINY CIRCLE

Women often come together to deal with specific problems and get things done. When a neighborhood starts to get shabby, they form a group to communicate with building owners about city codes and get the place cleaned up. If there isn't enough for teenagers to do in their small town, they put a group together to get a recreational center financed and built. The Destiny Circle does not deal with those agendas. It is devoted entirely to your personal journey. You are united with other women by your femaleness, roles in society, and commitment to exploring your spirituality and purpose.

Unlike a group you may form in church, the Destiny Circle

is not limited by the doctrine of a certain faith. It is not a place to discuss politics because the point is to share with others, not about others. This is where you discuss your soul's journey. In the Isis Circle we never discuss politics, money, or race because it never comes up. It's a personal space with a sister's agenda. Women who are facing a challenging situation want empathy, not sympathy. "How can I get through this? I haven't been here before." It's about safety for your soul.

SETTING UP YOUR DESTINY CIRCLE

Members. The longing you feel to connect to other women who are transitioning to a new season of life will guide you to members of your Destiny Circle. You probably already have one woman in mind, and aligning with her is the first step. Use your intuition as you discuss who comes to mind and write down the purpose of your Destiny Circle so that each potential member will understand. I recommend limiting the group to twelve or less so that each person will have an opportunity to talk at each meeting.

Time and place. While speaking to your potential members, ask about the most convenient time for a one- to one-and-a-half-hour meeting and take notes. When your list of members is complete, compare notes and find the common time frame that covers most and work from there. Next, decide how often you want to meet. Once a month is a good start and keeps the meetings far enough apart so that everyone will have new material to share. The confidential nature of the topics you will discuss calls for a private, comfortable space in which everyone can see each other, so hold your circle meeting in someone's home. Our Isis group met around my large, round dining room table, but sitting in a more informal way may work just as well.

Structure. Designate a timekeeper who will keep the flow going by keeping everyone to her allotted time. That amount of time will depend on the number in your group, of course. Ten minutes each may not sound like much, but if you have twelve members, ten minutes apiece will consume two hours. I suggest starting out with five- or six-minute timings. If you have a very small group, you could do two rounds.

Schedule the session so that there are fifteen minutes to settle in with refreshments before the meeting starts. Mark the opening of the circle with a moment of silence, prayer, or reading of a poem or other text that you have chosen to represent the journey that brought you together. You may decide to be specific about what each person should share, such as a conflict that is challenging her new priorities in the second half of life, or keep it open to any insight or concern about her personal journey. Establish the ground rules: no politics, current events, or town gossip. This is life journey time.

> *Your Destiny Circle will become the family of your second half of life, as vital as your biological family was in your first.*

After everyone has had their turn, the circle can break into a discussion on a topic that everyone agrees upon—if there is time. We rarely have time for discussion in the Isis Circle because most of the women have to get to work on a Friday morning, but when we do we often pick up on a subject that someone brought up in their individual time.

Privacy. Building trust and community requires that everything said at the Destiny Circle is confidential. Make this clear at the first meeting and with new members. Type up a sheet containing everyone's e-mail and other contact information and distribute it at the first meeting (or collect the information at the first meeting and distribute afterward). You may want to make a rule about e-mails: Some people do not appreciate receiving forwarded e-mails about "inspirational" subjects, for example.

Continuity. Schedule your next meeting at the end of each gathering or map out the next six months at the end of the first meeting.

A New Family

Your Destiny Circle will become the family of your second half of life, as vital as your biological family was in your first. And like family, you will feel closer to some members than others. I gravitated to a few close Isis members when I went through the loss of my parents and my brother. My entire sense of being a New Yorker had changed because I no longer had a member of my family to call or with whom to celebrate milestones and birthdays and share the city as our home. Knowing that I had an Isis sister to call helped me through that period like nothing else could. During our circle meetings, I was more careful about keeping everyone's timing in order so that I, as the facilitator, would have time to tell my story at the end. I had often skipped my time allotment in order to let someone speak a moment longer or encourage a short "bridge" discussion after someone shared a dramatic story.

Over the years, the sense of family has deepened. One of the women who was there at the beginning, a single mom and professional who was just going through a divorce and brought her daughter to the circle meetings, shared four years ago that her daughter was getting ready to go to college. We passed a plate around like she was our child. Now her daughter is home from college and brings some of her fellow graduates to the summer beach house gatherings. Watching her grow up added to our sense of family.

Working at the soul level, where you feel safe to describe and celebrate the most meaningful aspects of your journey as well as your struggles with obstacles from within and without, puts the Destiny Circle at the heart of your new life. You may become closer to Isis sisters than you are to members of your biological family. I have seen women blossom and friendships develop between the most unlikely people. They find healing in putting words to their experiences and listening to others. We need a place to share our deep stories and expand our awareness through the stories of others.

Your Destiny Circle will become part of your soul's DNA. Connecting with women who are on a similar path not only validates your process of becoming a Woman of Destiny but becomes a central part of the journey itself. The sacred initiation that we go through as we enter the second half of life deserves a passionate commitment and the support of like-minded women with a lifetime of experience and insights to share.

I wish you the journey of a lifetime and am grateful for the spirit of adventure, integrity, and purposefulness you bring to the world as you enter your new season. Now more than ever, we need your unique combination of intelligent, spiritual, intuitive, honorable, passionate, and well-honed gifts to lead us into a more balanced and joyful future.

DEBORAH, DREAMS, AND DESTINY

Not only do I advocate your taking a "selah," a pause in the action in which you can assess how your destiny will unfold, but I think transition is one of the gifts God gives us to begin to dream again. God puts a pause on our "play" button. Not rewind, not fast forward, but pause.

It is no accident that Deborah took time to rule under her palm tree. The mastering of her time management allowed her more time to think, to pray, and to dream. A Woman of Destiny finds and takes this time. She seizes it. She squeezes it.

Dreams do not have an expiration date. They may have been dormant, but dust them off and use this time to dream again. Do not be distracted, dissuaded, or detoured off your path. Your destiny is at stake.

It's interesting how people have become so used to "over-multitasking" that when we reduce the load on our plate or want to switch gears they call us "unstable" or ask, "So, what are you going to do now?" as though our entire identity is lost. Bishop TD Jakes calls this reassessment time "in between mountains." It is getting off one mountain long enough to determine which other ones we'd like to climb, if any or if at all. It is *not* the valley of the shadow of death, but between mountains or, as I like to say, "in between assignments." It is the place where we are waiting for our next marching orders from God. Each of us has at least one thing in this life that we are called and chosen to do like no one else.

I created this book from a very personal and professional perspective because I was, and continue to be, in transition as I wrote it. Clearly, I am "in between assignments." At the end of 2009, the beginning of my thirtieth year as a parish pastor in New York City, I made a choice to retire as senior pastor from one of my charges, the Bronx Christian Fellowship Church. I felt my duties, my assignment, and my mission had been fulfilled in that place. I had been there for fifteen years as the founding pastor and my vision had been realized. I believe that it's very important not to overstay your time in any one place, so even though I did not have a vision for beyond that time, I officially moved on.

Discernment is a spiritual gift that intuitively, instinctively, insightfully, and spiritually lets you know what you need to know, when to arrive and when to leave, when to enter, and when to stay away. I still have the pastorate of the Wall Street weekly congregation, three hundred dynamic men and women who meet downtown at lunchtime on Wednesdays. I am building a Women of Faith Center in Washington, D.C., and an annual conference/retreat for women leaders is still on my plate. But in spite of those continued and new roles, someone who had heard about my retirement from the church asked me, "So, what are you going to do now?" as though my Bronx pastorship was all that defined me.

My dear Women of Destiny, no more roles, no more drama—unless your dream is to be an actor. This is your divine denouement—your time to be at center stage of your own life. You are the writer of this episode. Do not let others take you through this transition. It is something only you and God can plan and experience. Transition is not a state of instability but a time of reassessing your abilities. Be unapologetic and unashamed. See yourself as *you* envision yourself, no one else, and *be* yourself.

Enjoy this time of transition. See it as a gift from the creator—time to think, dream, and pray again. Dare to live your life the way you'd like. Do not limit yourself. Be realistic about your capabilities, but dream big. It is no surprise to me that this book is being released in 2010, for not only does it celebrate a new chapter in our lives but also a new decade. Let this be the decade in which your dreams come true.

Our creator "is able to do exceeding abundantly above all that we ask or think" (Ephesians 3:20, KJV), which means taking us *beyond* where we are to where we desire to be. The new worlds, new realms, and new places we've dreamed of are waiting for us to arrive. And surrounding them are even more experiences and places we have not yet envisioned, ready to fling open their doors to us.

This is your moment. Declare with me: "My destiny is unfolding *now*!"

FORMING YOUR DESTINY CIRCLE
√ **CHECKLIST**

___ Team up with one friend to launch my Destiny Circle and make a list of potential members.

___ Create a mission statement for the circle.

___ Invite potential members and describe the group according to the mission statement.

___ Schedule the first Destiny Circle and choose a way to open each meeting (moment of silence, line from a poem, prayer, etc.).

___ Print out a contact list of members and distribute.

___ Announce ground rules at the first meeting, including number of minutes for each person to speak, e-mail rules (if any), and confidentiality.

MY PILLAR IV CONTRACT WITH DESTINY

As I approach transition into a new chapter of my life, I am grateful for this opportunity to bring my experience, wisdom, heart, and soul to my community and my world. Everything that has happened to me up to now has been a preparation for this new season. The timing is perfect. I may never know all the effects of my words and actions as they ripple throughout the world, but I say and do them in a spirit of generosity, love, and respect for all. As a Woman of Destiny, I am strengthened in everything I do by my Destiny Circle, which unites my kindred spirits in an environment of trust, inspiration, and joy.

Afterwords

PRAYERS AND MEDITATIONS FOR THE WOMAN OF DESTINY

PRAYERS

Making Goals

Behold, I will do a new thing; now it shall spring forth
(Isaiah 43:19a, KJV).

Today I place myself in the hands of the Divine, for I know that my destiny has been mapped out, pre-planned, pre-determined, pre-destined. I am ready for that which is new. Help me, O Lord, to discover my unique feminine gifts, talent, and potential. When you created me, you blew into me your very breath and created me in your image. May I walk as a woman in your wisdom, your image, and with your insight. Here I am; mold me, lead me, use me where you see the need for what I have. Let me be MAP'ped (Mentored, Advocated for, and Prepared) by thee as I seek the map, the way, the road for my new life.

Amen.

New Beginnings

This is the day which the Lord has made, we will rejoice and be glad in it. (Psalm 118:24, KJV).

The psalmist declares that we are invited to seize the brand-new day with joy and gladness. God, as I prepare to set new goals, may I not only see this as a new day but also as a new beginning. This is truly the first day of the rest of my life. Help me leave anything and everything that is old in the past in order to embrace and encounter that which is new. I am your daughter of destiny—destined for greatness and ready for forgiveness so that anything that blocks or clutters my new openings will be out of my way.

A new chapter now begins. I am ready to turn the page as I turn over a new leaf. May the seeds you sowed into my life now blossom. May I be deeply rooted in thee, ever sprouting, ever springing forth with new, amazing life and energy.

Amen.

Finding Opportunities in Tough Times

Lo, I am with you always, even unto the end of the world (Matthew 28:20b, KJV).

Pray without ceasing. In everything give thanks: for this is the will of God (1 Thessalonians 5:17–18a, KJV).

It is good to know that the Savior is here with and for me. Some days I feel so all alone, as though I have to really "tough out" the difficult days.

This fast-paced life has replaced great friendships. I ask to bond with my friends again, and if they have moved on, I ask for new ones. I realize I cannot microwave relationships but must place them on "slow cook" and allow them to simmer.

Sometimes I feel like Naomi, in a strange place and a strange land. I need a Ruth, a sister to walk beside me. But most of all, Lord, I need you to be my friend and guide. Teach me how to stop and listen for your voice and to your voice. Thank you, because today I really need it.

Amen.

Dear Lord,

I thank you for life and I thank you that I have YOU to come to in my time of need. "Create in me a clean heart, O God; and renew a right spirit within me" (Psalm 51:10).

I come today knowing that there is nothing that I go through alone, but that you are here with me. You are making provision for the vision. You are replacing the scars with stars.

Not only are you able to keep me from falling, but also from falling apart. I need you to be the glue that keeps the pieces from scattering and the wind beneath my wings that keeps me from shattering. Thanks, dear God; I feel better already.

Amen.

A Respectful Life

**Do to others what you would have them do to you
(Matthew 7:12).**

In every faith there is some version of the Golden Rule as written in Matthew. Today I ask for and give respect. I am intentional about speaking to others and greeting them with a "good morning." I am respectful of others' time and realize that my promptness is important, for no one is obligated to give me any part of his day or her life. Teach me to be thankful and respectful to all whom I encounter, my family, my friends, my co-workers, and my co-sojourners. This is my prayer, this day and always.

Amen.

Finding Strength

**Mine eyes have seen the King, the Lord of Hosts
(Isaiah 6:5, KJV).**

Dear God,

As Isaiah the prophet's eyes were opened to see that his strength was not dependent on a king, but rather on you, may I, too, find that inner strength and peace to give me the vision, vitality, and victory I need to go forth. As your angels touched his lips, may your angels touch my heart and my being, that my will and yours will be one. Give me this day my daily bread and lead me not into temptation, but ever closer toward you. O, Lord, you are my strength and my redeemer.

Amen.

Trusting

He who trusts in the Lord will prosper
(Proverbs 28:25, NIV).

Rock my boat today, dear God. As your disciples were told to go into deeper waters, may I, too, leave the familiar, the shallow, and begin to discover parts of this ocean of life I've never known. I'm ready to take a risk. I'm ready to jump off the diving board. I realize that you have given me everything I need to go forward. Let me swim out to meet my new adventures.

Amen.

Gratitude

The apostle Paul declared, "I have learned, in whatsoever
state I am, to be content" (Philippians 4:11b, Douay).

Paul learned that there was work to be done wherever he landed and that it was preordained by God for him to be there. In other words, this was God's will for him. Too many spend time complaining and moaning. Gratitude is so much easier and even triggers an amazing response in my body. That's why Paul also wrote, "In every thing give thanks: for this is the will of God" (1 Thessalonians 5:18a, KJV). Gratitude costs nothing but gains us so much. Thank you—for my life, my health, my wealth of knowledge and my ability to have the inclination to give you thanks.

Amen.

Affirmation: Today I write a letter to those in my life who have brought me great joy and simply say, "Thank you."

A New Spark

**I have come that they might have life, and that they might
have it more abundantly (John 10:10, KJV).**
Life is meant to be abundant in all areas. Today, I decide what I want.

I believe I can have it.
I believe I deserve it.
I believe it is possible for me.
I am a magnet for the magnificent.
I am anointed to be me.
I am actualizing abundance.
I am ignited, excited, delighted.
Amen.

MEDITATIONS

First Day of the New Year

Today is the first day of a new year and the first day of the rest of my life.

I have left everything and anything that is old in the old year. I must close the last chapter so the new chapter can begin.

Today I turn the page. I turn over a new leaf and begin to work toward my DESTINY.

Catching Up with Myself: "Selah"

In his wisdom, the psalmist put a "selah," a pause mark in his music, so that he could rest up to enjoy what he had written, the music God had put in him. Some days you just need to catch up with yourself. No more of you to anyone, for anyone else—but YOU.

"Me, myself, and I," the kids used to say in the playground. Today, find some ground to play on, pray on, stay on, and weigh in with yourself.

The rat race is over. Everything and everyone has to be put on hold. Remember the song from the late Sammy Davis, Jr., with the words, "Stop the world, I want to get off." Today give yourself permission to "get off" and "go within" deeply to that place, that space where no one else can enter. This is God's day, but it is also YOUR day. Catch up, breathe. *Selah*.

This Is the Day the Lord Hath Made for Me

The matinee is over. The main feature is about to come on. It's YOU!! Seasoned. Reasoned. Ready. Restored. Be the star in your own show, your one-woman show.

No extras. No understudies. No set. You're SET.

The curtain is about to rise and what will they see? What will they hear?

"I'm coming out, I want the world to know!"

Catch Your Breath

EXHILIRATION! EXHAUSTION! EXHALE!

There are times when even the best multitaskers on earth get tired.

Can you imagine how much Deborah had on her plate?

We have to acknowledge that there are no Superwoman capes. We just have to take off the garments we wear to work and play. It's great to have wonder-filled, fruitful days, but it's also important to stop long enough to enjoy what you've experienced and exhale to get a new breath.

The psalmist declared, "Let every thing that hath breath praise the Lord" (Psalm 150:6), but you have to have some breath left. Perhaps you haven't made merry music in a while because you've not stopped long enough. It's time to exhale.

Her-story

March is Women's History Month, but I believe whenever and wherever there is a woman doing something of significance, it is her day, her week, her year—her-story.

Declare this day as your day, your week, your month. Honor your femaleness, your femininity wrapped in and insulated with divinity. Plan your Destiny circle this month and invite all your sister friends to join you in playing and praying.

Plan a movie night, a dinner out, a comedy club, a walk, or a day with destined women.

Laugh, love, let go.

A merry heart is good for the soul!

Recommended Reading

BOOKS TO ENLIGHTEN, MOTIVATE, AND INSPIRE

Goal-Making/Claiming Your Gifts

Linda Ellis Eastman, *Women's Survival Guide for Overcoming Obstacles, Transition & Change* (Professional Woman Publishing, 2007)

James Hillman, *The Soul's Code: In Search of Character and Calling* (Grand Central Publishing, 1997)

Maureen Murdock, *The Heroine's Journey* (Shambhala, 1990)

Rick Warren, *The Purpose Driven Life* (Zondervan, 2007)

Prayer

Evelyn Christenson, *What Happens When Women Pray* (Victor Books, 1977)

Suzan Johnson Cook, *Sister to Sister: Devotions for and from African American Women* (Judson Press, 1995)

Larry Dossey, *Healing Words: The Power of Prayer and the Practice of Medicine* (HarperCollins, 1993)

———. *Prayer Is Good Medicine* (HarperOne, 1997)

Richard Foster, *Prayer: Finding the Heart's True Home* (HarperOne, 1992)

Jonathan Graf, *The Power of Personal Prayer: Learning to Pray with Faith and Purpose* (NavPress, 2002)

Steve Harper, *Talking in the Dark: Praying When Life Doesn't Make Sense* (Upper Room, 2007)

James Houston, *The Transforming Power of Prayer: Deepening Your Friendship with God* (Lion, 1989)

W. Bingham Hunter, *The God Who Hears* (InterVarsity Press, 1986)

Bill Hybels, *Too Busy Not to Pray* (InterVarsity Press, 1998)

Peter Kreeft, *Prayer: The Great Conversation* (Ignatius Press, 1991)

Roy Lawrence, *How to Pray When Life Hurts* (InterVarsity Press, 1993)

Paul E. Miller, *A Praying Life: Connecting with God in a Distracting World* (NavPress, 2009)

J. Oswald Sanders, *Prayer Power Unlimited* (Discovery House, 1997)

John White, *Daring to Draw Near* (InterVarsity Press, 1977)

Miriam Therese Winter, *WomanPrayer, WomanSong* (Wipf & Stock, 2008)

———. *WomanWitness* (Crossroad, 1992); includes a prayer and psalm on Deborah

Philip Yancey, *Prayer: Does It Make Any Difference?* (Zondervan, 2006)

David Yount, *Breaking Through God's Silence* (Simon & Schuster, 1996)

Inspiration

Jack Canfield, *Chicken Soup for the Woman's Soul* (Health Communications, 1996)

———. *Chicken Soup to Inspire a Woman's Soul: Stories Celebrating the Wisdom, Fun and Freedom of Midlife* (Health Communications, 2004)

———. *A Second Chicken Soup for the Woman's Soul* (Health Communications, 1998)

Suzan Johnson Cook, *Too Blessed to Be Stressed: Words of Wisdom for Women on the Move* (Thomas Nelson, 1998)

Cynthia Kersey, *Unstoppable: 45 Powerful Stories of Perseverance and Triumph from People Just Like You* (Sourcebooks, 1998)

Anne Lamott, *Grace (Eventually): Thoughts on Faith* (Riverhead, 2008)

Felicity Leng, *Invincible Spirits: A Thousand Years of Women's Spiritual Writings* (Wm. B. Eerdmans Publishing, 2007)

A. Mikaelian, *Women Who Mean Business: Success Stories of Women over Forty* (William Morrow, 1999)

Richard Thomas, *It's A Miracle: Real-life Inspirational Stories* (Random House, 2002)

Societies That Honor Women of Destiny

Heidi Goettner-Abendroth, *Societies of Peace: Matriarchies Past, Present and Future* (Inanna Publications, 2009)

Peggy Reeves Sanday, *Women at the Center: Life In a Modern Matriarchy* (Cornell University Press, 2004)

Your Best Work Is Still Ahead: The New Brain Research

Eric P. Jensen, *7 Amazing Discoveries: Practical Applications of New Brain Research* (DVD, Corwin Press, 2006)

Matthew Macdonald, *Your Brain: The Missing Manual* (Pogue Press, 2008)

John Medina, *Brain Rules: 12 Principles for Surviving and Thriving at Work, Home, and School* (Pear Press, 2009)

John J. Ratey, *Spark*: *the Revolutionary New Science of Exercise and the Brain* (Little, Brown, 2008)

Richard Restak, *Mozart's Brain and the Fighter Pilot: Unleashing Your Brain's Potential* (Three Rivers Press, 2002)

———. *Think Smart: A Neuroscientist's Prescription for Improving Your Brain's Performance* (Riverhead, 2009)

Getting Your House in Order

Antoinette Babek, *Women Empowering Themselves: A Financial Survival Guide* (Dog Ear Publishing, 2009)

Candace Bahr, *It's More Than Money—It's Your Life!* (Wiley, 2003)

Janet Bodnar: *Kiplinger's Money Smart Women* (Kaplan Business, 2006)

Suze Orman, *Women & Money* (Spiegel & Grau, 2010)

About the Author

Reverend Dr. Suzan Johnson Cook—Dr. Sujay—is an author, educator, former White House adviser, public speaker, preacher, and faith adviser to political leaders and celebrities, recently described in *The New York Times* as "Billy Graham and Oprah rolled into one." She is known as "the Wall Street pastor" for her weekly lunchtime worship services in downtown Manhattan and was named by *Ebony* magazine as one of the nation's top fifteen women in ministry, by *Time Out* as one of New York's top five preachers, and by Dr. Gardner C. Taylor in *Time* magazine as the "Harriet Tubman for women." Creator of Harlem Halleluiah at the Apollo Theater and Wonderful Washington Worship in the nation's capital, Dr. Sujay is one of American's most innovative clergywomen.

Dr. Sujay's nine books include the three bestsellers *Moving Up* (Doubleday, 2008), *Live Like You're Blessed* (Doubleday, 2006), and *Sister to Sister* (Judson), and *Too Blessed to Be Stressed* (Nelson, 1998), *A New Dating Attitude—Getting Ready for the Mate God Has for You* (Zondervan, 2000), and *The Sister's Rules for Ministry* (Word, 2003).

Dr. Sujay was the first African-American woman to become a senior pastor in the two-hundred-year history of American Baptist Churches of the USA, the first woman president of the ten-thousand-member Hampton University Ministers' Conference, the first woman appointed chaplain of the New York City Police Department, and the first woman Baptist minister to receive a White House fellowship.

Recently retired from the Bronx Christian Fellowship Church after thirty years of serving inner-city churches, she now pastors the Wall Street lunchtime congregation and is the founder of Wisdom Women Worldwide, an international faith center for women leaders.

A faculty member and former fellow of Harvard University, Dr. Sujay received a doctor of ministry degree from United Theological Seminary (Dayton, Ohio), a master of divinity from Union Theological Seminary (New York City), and a master of arts from Columbia University. She and her family live in New York City.